ILIAD 54

ILIAD 54

Reflections and Translations on Homer's *Iliad*

PETER ARCESE

ATHANATA ARTS, LTD
Garden City, New York

Copyright © 2025 Peter Arcese
All photographs, English text, and translations are the original work of the author and are protected under United States and international copyright laws. All rights reserved.

Athanata Arts, Ltd.
Garden City, New York
Published and printed in the United States of America

www.athanata.com

Portions of the Greek text are adapted from *Homeri Opera* (Oxford: Oxford University Press, 1920), made available through the Perseus Digital Library under a Creative Commons Attribution-ShareAlike 3.0 United States License.

ISBN (hardcover) 979-8-9919585-1-6
ISBN (paperback) 979-8-9919585-2-3

First edition

Library of Congress Catalog Control Number: 2025943276

Billowing smoke swears an oath to the city's defeat,
shockwaves of ruin stagger crumbling rubble, while
embers fade in the thick breath of scorched wealth.

— Aeschlyus, *Agamemnon*

Note to the Reader

On September 11, 2024, I realized there were fifty-four days until Election Day. The same number of days Homer chose to narrate in the *Iliad*.

I began a countdown. Each day I selected a passage from the epic and paired it with a photograph from my archive, along with a brief reflection and my own translation.

Homer used fifty-four days to contain a war that spanned ten years. This book gathers fifty-four moments from those days. The sequence is not chronological. I chose each passage as it came to mind, one day after another.

ILIAD 54

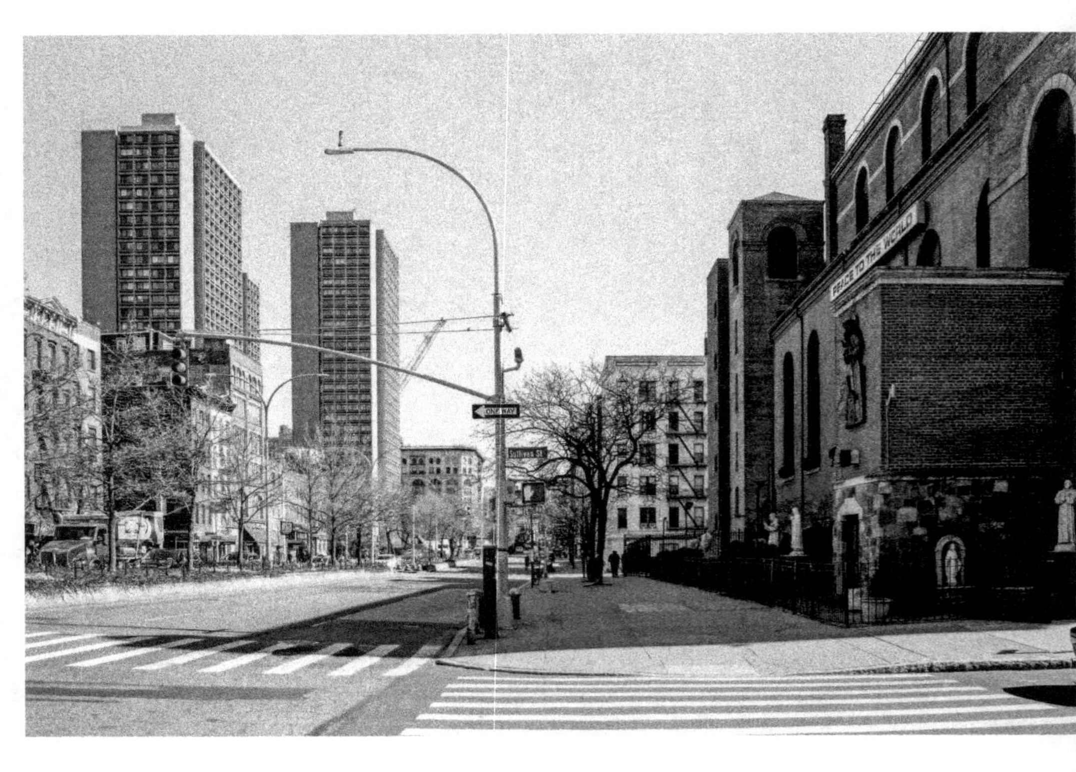
ONE WAY
PEACE TO THE WORLD

I was living on Bleecker Street in the building tucked just visibly between the towers on the left. As I lay in bed, I heard an unusual sound and thought of my aunt Julia's story. About the plane that crashed into the Empire State Building in 1945.

I walked into the living room. As the second tower fell, I heard the collective gasp of a small crowd gathered seventeen floors below.

That was Troy — not here.

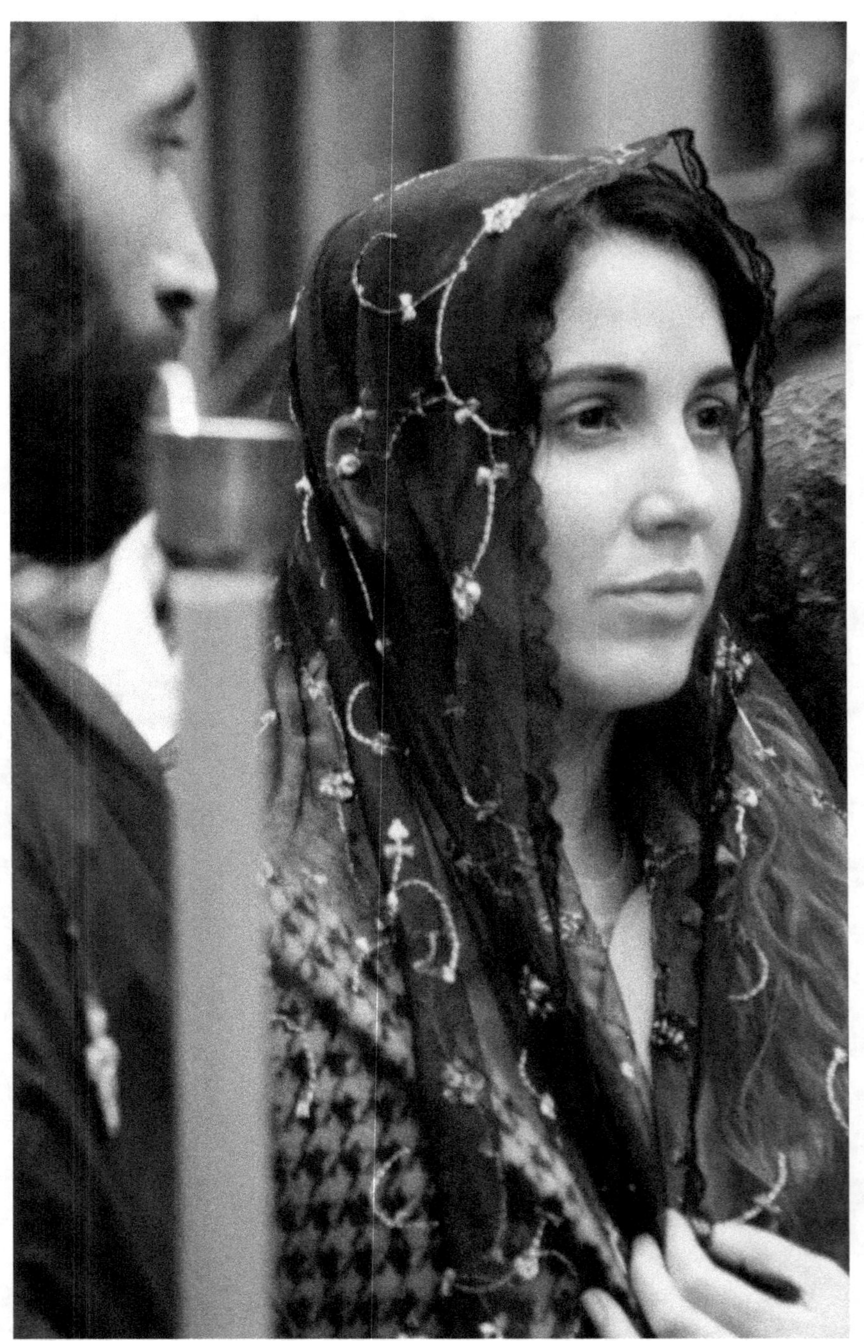

54

Before the sun set on the first day, Achilles watched the two he loved walk away along the beach. Patroclus, was he gently grasping her wrist? Or did she allow him to lead her, her hand in his?

Briseis watched, too. She kept looking back as she stepped farther away, closer to the horizon. She kept looking at the son of Peleus standing in the deepening shadow of the ships.

That moment when he no longer sees the color of her eyes is when sorrow blends with rage and becomes ruin — *até*.

ὣς φάτο, Πάτροκλος δὲ φίλῳ ἐπεπείθεθ᾽ ἑταίρῳ,
ἐκ δ᾽ ἄγαγε κλισίης Βρισηΐδα καλλιπάρῃον,
δῶκε δ᾽ ἄγειν: τὼ δ᾽ αὖτις ἴτην παρὰ νῆας Ἀχαιῶν:
ἣ δ᾽ ἀέκουσ᾽ ἅμα τοῖσι γυνὴ κίεν: αὐτὰρ Ἀχιλλεὺς
δακρύσας ἑτάρων ἄφαρ ἕζετο νόσφι λιασθείς,
θῖν᾽ ἔφ᾽ ἁλὸς πολιῆς, ὁρόων ἐπ᾽ ἀπείρονα πόντον:

So he spoke, and Patroclus obeyed the command
of his friend and comrade, leading Briseis,
fair-cheeked in her beauty, out from the tent and
gave her to be taken away. So the two walked back
alongside the Achaean ships, as she followed, unwillingly.

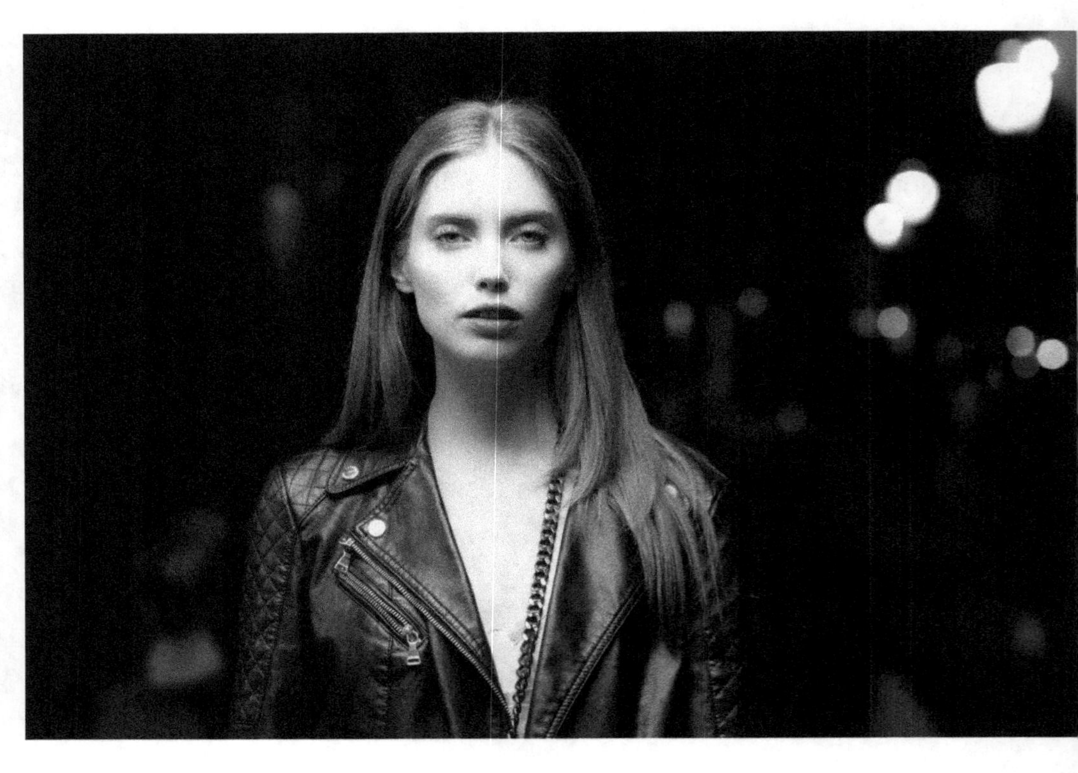

53

You are not supposed to see her.

Homer won't let you look directly at her. You have to follow her through the eyes of the elders as she appears. You are compelled to watch as she walks by you, along the cyclopean walls to survey the field of the Argive forces spread on the plains below.

For as long as the story remains the same, you have to picture Helen for yourself. The picture will not remain the same because your vision will change.

τοῖοι ἄρα Τρώων ἡγήτορες ἦντ᾽ ἐπὶ πύργῳ.
οἳ δ᾽ ὡς οὖν εἴδονθ᾽ Ἑλένην ἐπὶ πύργον ἰοῦσαν,
ἦκα πρὸς ἀλλήλους ἔπεα πτερόεντ᾽ ἀγόρευον:
'οὐ νέμεσις Τρῶας καὶ ἐϋκνήμιδας Ἀχαιοὺς
τοιῇδ᾽ ἀμφὶ γυναικὶ πολὺν χρόνον ἄλγεα πάσχειν:

So the wise elders of Troy sat along the tower heights.
And when they saw Helen approaching along the parapet,
they spoke to each other in hushed tones with winged words:
There's no wonder and no blame that the Trojans and
well-armed Achaeans would suffer long for such a woman.

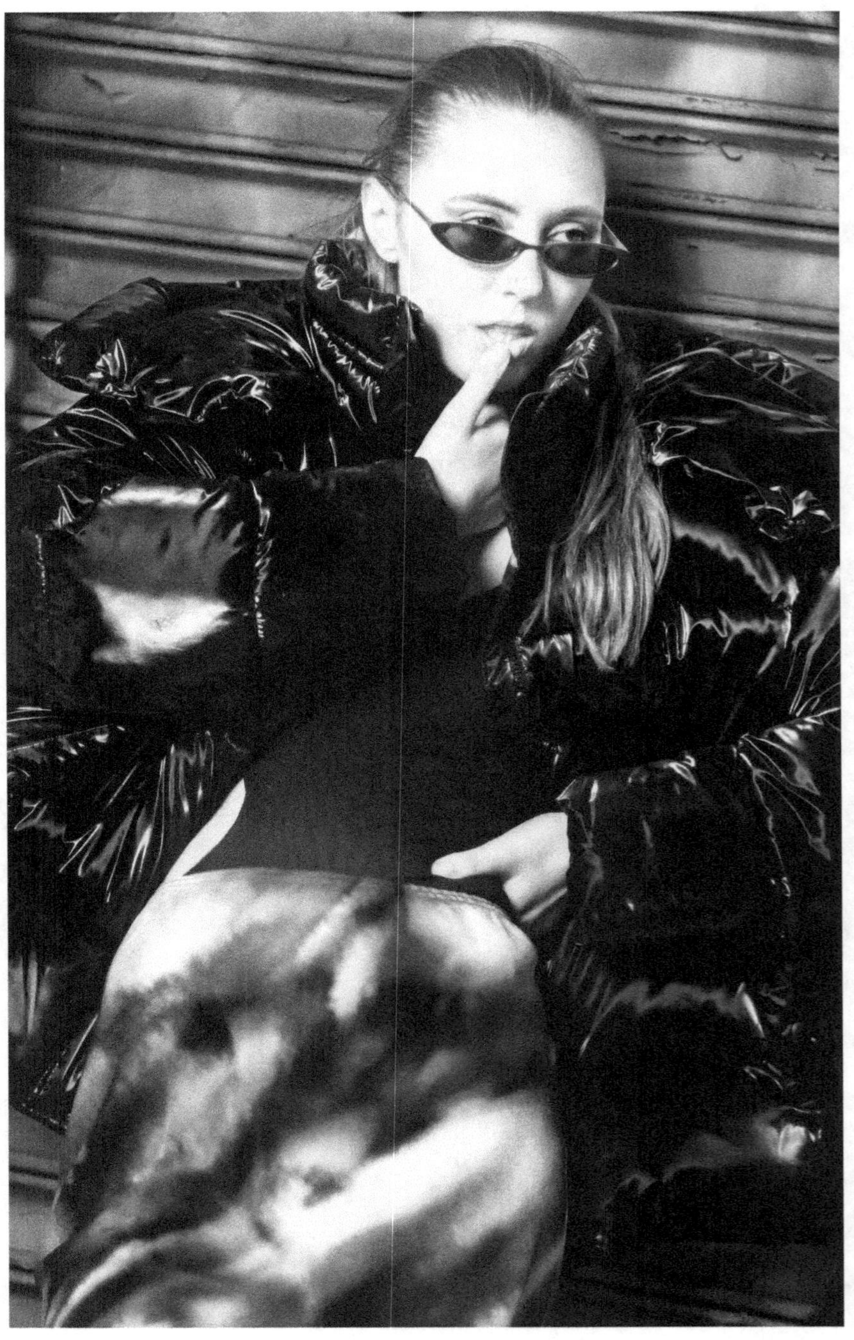

52

It’s a cutting word, a harsh word. Homer has Helen speak it against herself. The lexicon has an entry for *kunopis:*

κυνώπης dog-eyed

Most translators agree that its sense is "shameless." But their choices range from "dog-face" (Wilson), to "whore" (Fagles), to "bitch" (Mitchell).

Helen is standing next to Priam when she castigates herself. Priam speaks gently in return, offering her absolution. Neither condemnation nor ambiguity.

Place the blame on the gods, he tells her. All of the blame.

τοῦτο δέ τοι ἐρέω ὅ μ᾽ ἀνείρεαι ἠδὲ μεταλλᾷς:
οὗτός γ᾽ Ἀτρεΐδης εὐρὺ κρείων Ἀγαμέμνων,
ἀμφότερον βασιλεύς τ᾽ ἀγαθὸς κρατερός τ᾽ αἰχμητής:
δαὴρ αὖτ᾽ ἐμὸς ἔσκε κυνώπιδος, εἴ ποτ᾽ ἔην γε.

Let me tell you, I can answer your question. That man is the son of Atreus, the powerful Agamemnon, both king and warrior — he is my husband's brother, once my kin by law, shameless bitch that I am, or ever was.

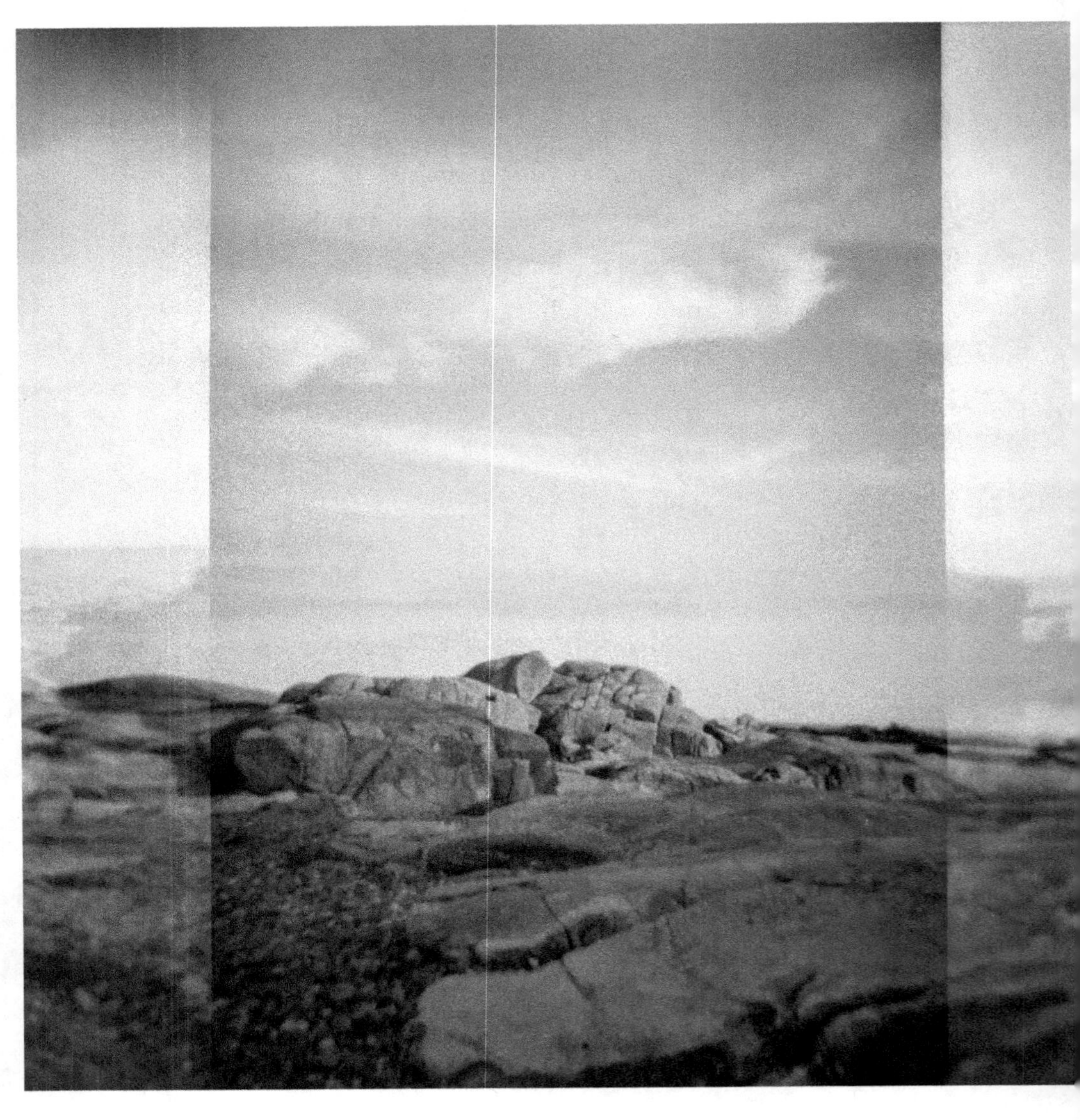

51

Nothing matters now that Briseis is sequestered in Agamemnon's tent.

Chryseis never looked back as Agamemnon's ship returned her to Apollo and her father. Achilles withdraws into the fading light to sit on the rocky shore and calls out for his mother.

Freud tried to explain the "oceanic feeling" as a remnant of infancy. The infant cries and immediately is soothed by the breast. The infant and the breast are one. Only when the breast is withdrawn does the pain of separation become reality. And the oceanic feeling becomes the echo of that time before — of an endless oneness — or before there was anyone else in the world to walk away.

καρπαλίμως δ' ἀνέδυ πολιῆς ἁλὸς ἠΰτ' ὀμίχλη,
καί ῥα πάροιθ' αὐτοῖο καθέζετο δάκρυ χέοντος,

All at once, she emerged from the gray sea like a mist, and set herself down next to him as his tears flowed.

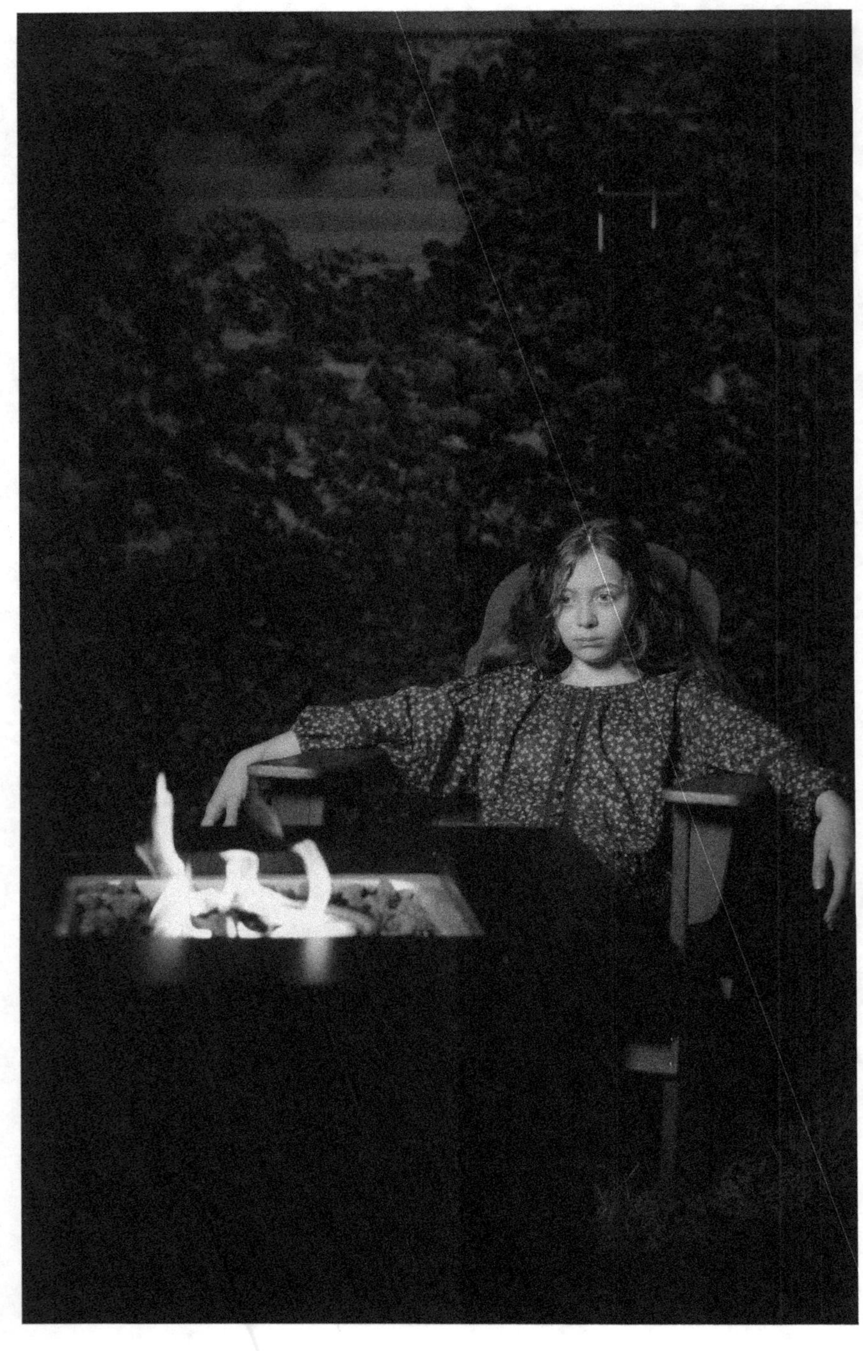

50

During the past year we have become accustomed to the domesticated fire pit. We sit by the propane-fueled flames, nestled into the parcel of our suburban lot.

The night that surrounds us is raw but tamed. Ivy crawls on the garage wall and spills across the lawn in the dark. Landscapers come every Tuesday to trim the grass surrounding our freshly painted Adirondack chairs.

In the tenth year of the war, before the trick of the horse, the watchfires and the campfires burned all night on the plain beside the river Xanthus.

χίλι' ἄρ' ἐν πεδίῳ πυρὰ καίετο, πὰρ δὲ ἑκάστῳ
εἵατο πεντήκοντα σέλᾳ πυρὸς αἰθομένοιο.
ἵπποι δὲ κρῖ λευκὸν ἐρεπτόμενοι καὶ ὀλύρας
ἑσταότες παρ' ὄχεσφιν ἐΰθρονον Ἠῶ μίμνον.

A thousand fires burned on the plain, and by each one fifty men sat in the glow of the blazing flame, while their horses fed on white barley and spelt, standing beside the chariots, waiting for Dawn to mount her lustrous throne.

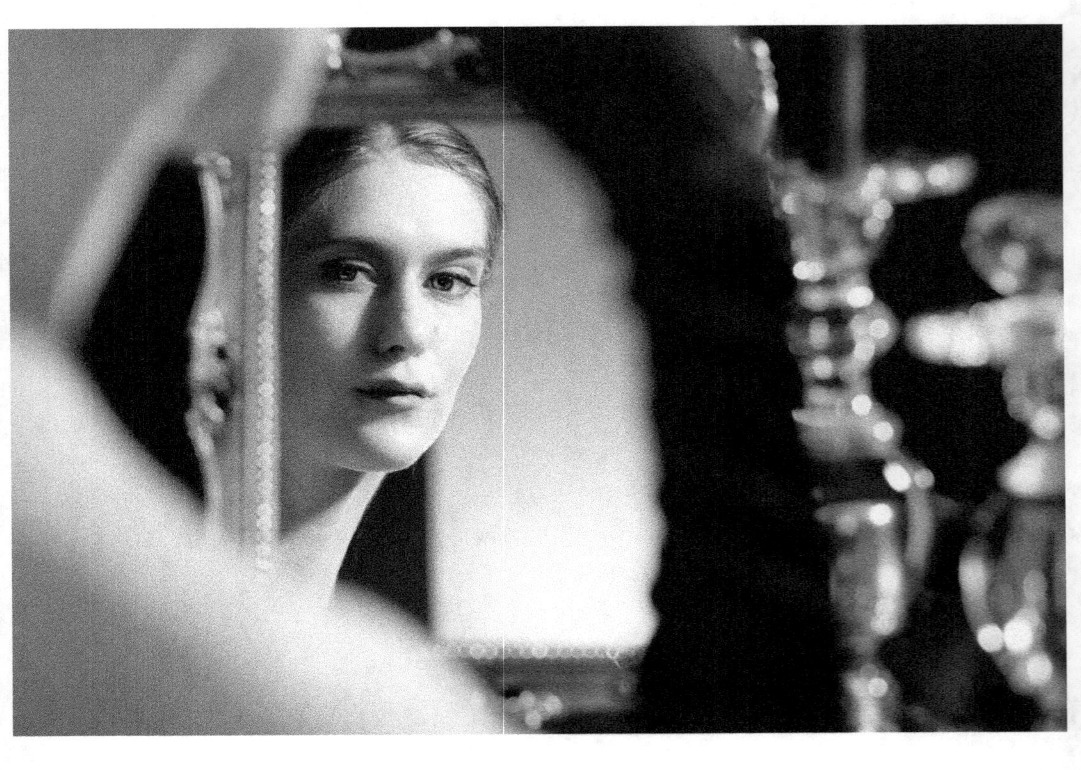

49

There is a rhythm to each day from the sparkling daylight to dusk. Menelaus strikes Paris's helmet so hard that his sword shatters. Enraged, he grabs the helmet and drags Paris, choking him with its leather strap.

Aprhodite swiftly saves her darling. Paris will not die that day. She lifts him in a mist and sets him, magically refreshed, safely in his lofty bedroom. Menelaus is left on the field below, holding an empty helmet glittering in the sun with a broken strap.

The scene changes, and Aphrodite summons Helen to the prince's bedroom, threatening her with death if she resists. It is evening when Helen steps in.

τῇ δ' ἄρα δίφρον ἑλοῦσα φιλομειδὴς Ἀφροδίτη
ἀντί' Ἀλεξάνδροιο θεὰ κατέθηκε φέρουσα:
ἔνθα κάθιζ' Ἑλένη κούρη Διὸς αἰγιόχοιο
ὄσσε πάλιν κλίνασα, πόσιν δ' ἠνίπαπε μύθῳ:

And Aphrodite, who loves laughter and smiles,
took a chair and set it down for Helen across from
Alexander. And there she sat, the daughter of
aegis-bearing Zeus, her eyes turned away from him.

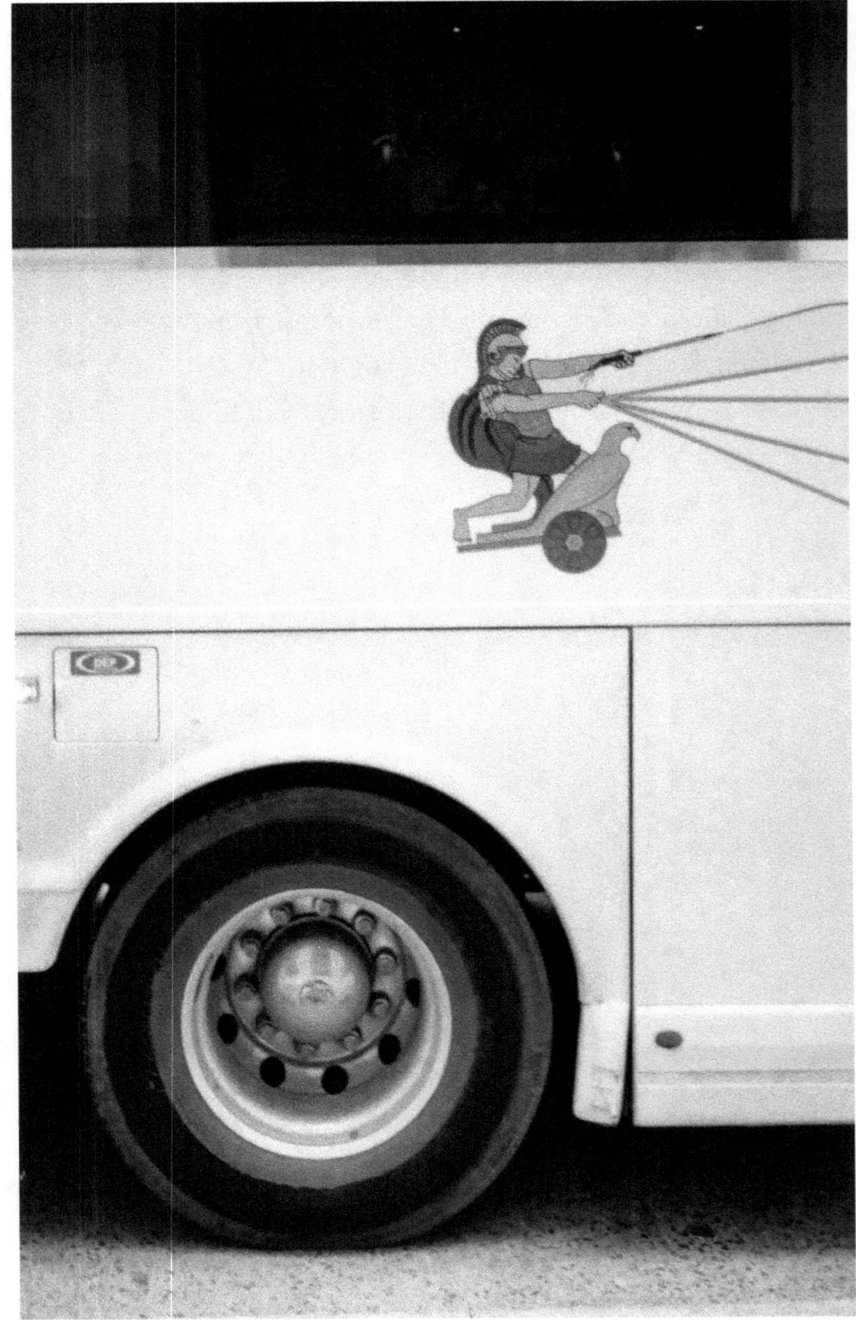

48

Before we witness the bloodiest scenes between Hector and Achilles, we watch as Diomedes wounds both Aphrodite and Ares. The gods suffer wounds, but they do not die. One of Homer's greatest gifts to his audience was to let them hear how the gods suffer, too.

. . . εἶθαρ δὲ δόρυ χροὸς ἀντετόρησεν
ἀμβροσίου διὰ πέπλου, ὅν οἱ Χάριτες κάμον αὐταί,
πρυμνὸν ὕπερ θέναρος: ῥέε δ᾽ ἄμβροτον αἷμα θεοῖο
ἰχώρ, οἷός πέρ τε ῥέει μακάρεσσι θεοῖσιν:
οὐ γὰρ σῖτον ἔδουσ᾽, οὐ πίνουσ᾽ αἴθοπα οἶνον,
τοὔνεκ᾽ ἀναίμονές εἰσι καὶ ἀθάνατοι καλέονται.

And straightaway, the spear pierced her tender skin, tearing the divinely delicate robe crafted by the Graces themselves, where the palm swells beneath the thumb, and immortal blood, ichor, flowed, which runs through the veins of the blessed gods — since they neither eat bread nor drink gleaming wine, so they are bloodless, and so are called deathless.

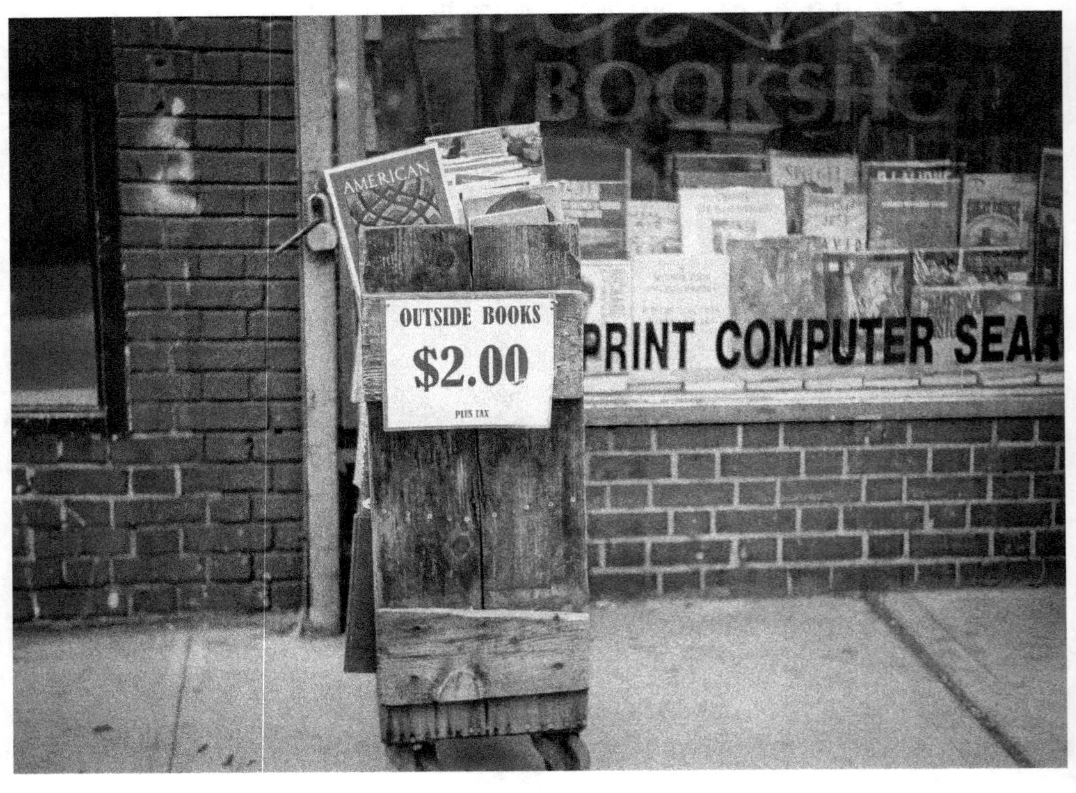
BOOKSHO
AMERICAN
OUTSIDE BOOKS
$2.00
PLUS TAX
PRINT COMPUTER SEAR

47

There is one tree — a pin oak (*quercus palustris*) — that I walk beneath every morning on my way to the coffee shop. For the past three days, I've stepped between handfuls of its fallen leaves, already dry, brittle, and brown.

I keep an edition of *Leaves of Grass* beside my bed.

When Glaucus is challenged by Diomedes, the son of Hippolochus responds with one of the most famous of Homeric similies.

οἵη περ φύλλων γενεὴ τοίη δὲ καὶ ἀνδρῶν.
φύλλα τὰ μέν τ᾽ ἄνεμος χαμάδις χέει, ἄλλα δέ θ᾽ ὕλη
τηλεθόωσα φύει, ἔαρος δ᾽ ἐπιγίγνεται ὥρη:
ὣς ἀνδρῶν γενεὴ ἣ μὲν φύει ἣ δ᾽ ἀπολήγει.

As with generations of leaves, so it is with men.
Some the wind sweeps to the ground, while the burgeoning forest sprouts new as the season turns to Spring; and so with generations of men, one blooms, the other fades.

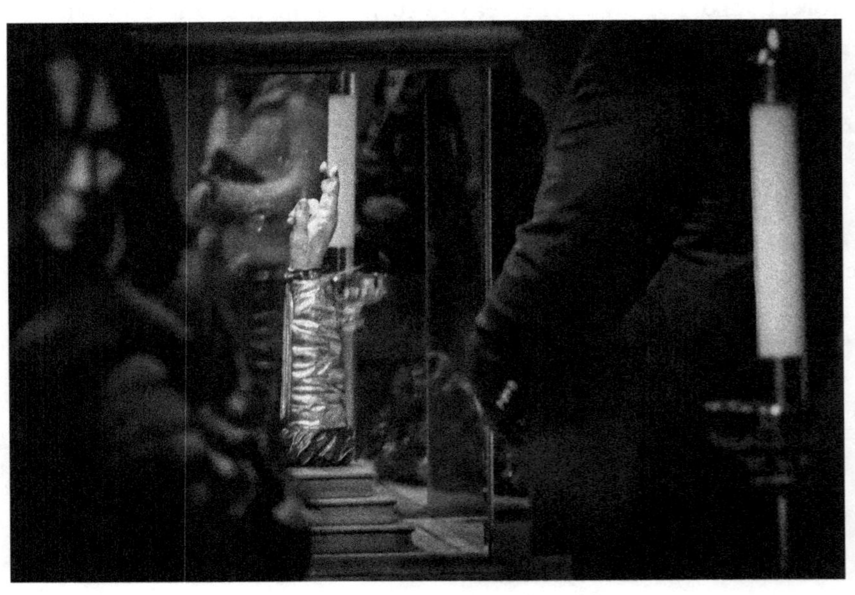

46

Agamemnon had made a terrible mistake, testing the army's resolve by telling them that the nine years of their war effort was a hopeless humiliation.

Odysseus, although widely praised as a "sweet-talker" (Hēduepēs), promptly took the scepter from Agamemnon's hands to pummel would-be deserters.

αὐτὸς δ' Ἀτρεΐδεω Ἀγαμέμνονος ἀντίος ἐλθὼν
δέξατό οἱ σκῆπτρον πατρώϊον ἄφθιτον αἰεί:
σὺν τῷ ἔβη κατὰ νῆας Ἀχαιῶν χαλκοχιτώνων.

And he himself came face to face with Atreides Agamemnon and took up from him the ancestral, eternal scepter, and with it swept along the ships of the bronze-clad Achaeans.

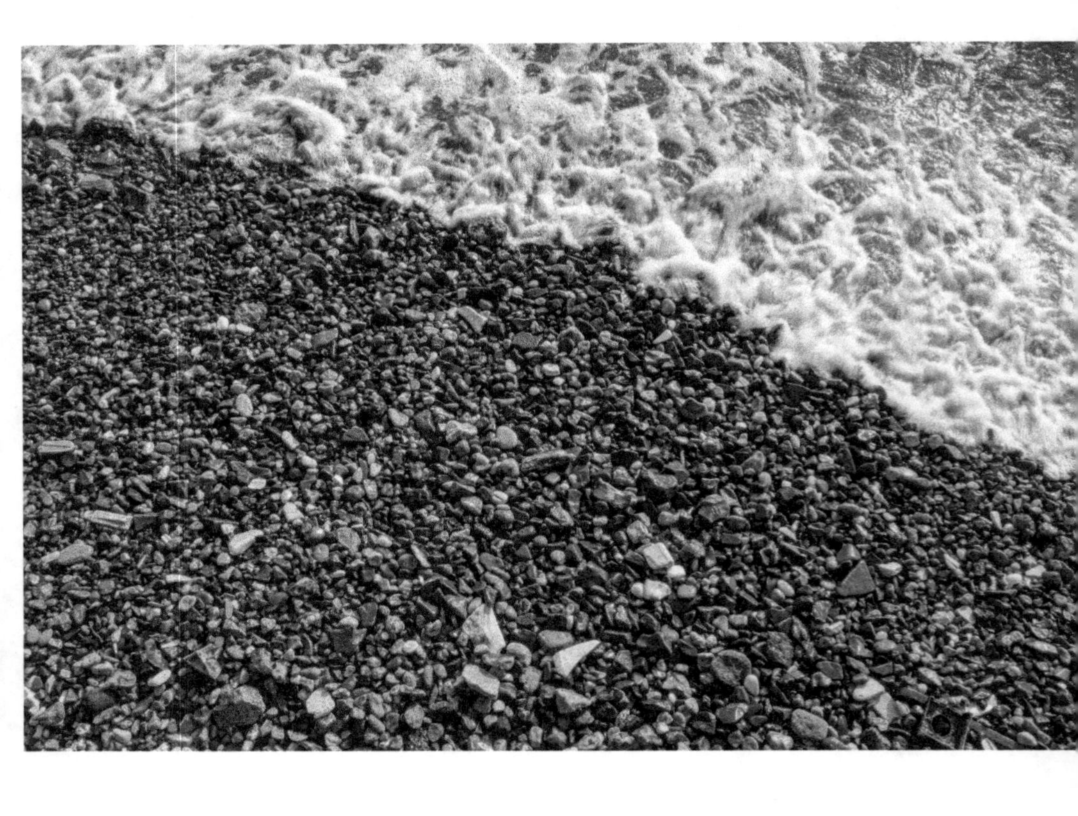

45

Agamemnon admits his inhuman rage. Not an apology, but an offer to buy back Achilles. An excess of riches to make amends, to restore the stolen honor by bestowing gift upon gift. Tripods, gold, cauldrons, stallions. Briseis, too (untouched, he insists). Finally, Agamemnon adds one of his own daughters to the offer — whichever of three, no bride-price required.

Achilles has been singing, passing the time as Patroclus sits silently across from him. Odysseus arrives and Achilles sets down his lyre to listen to the bribe. It is a lengthy presentation, worthy of a king's magnanimous promises.

The thought in reply comes quickly. *Not for all the world . . .*

ταῦτά κέ οἱ τελέσαιμι μεταλήξαντι χόλοιο.
δμηθήτω: Ἀΐδης τοι ἀμείλιχος ἠδ᾽ ἀδάμαστος,
τοὔνεκα καί τε βροτοῖσι θεῶν ἔχθιστος ἁπάντων:

All these things I will offer him in satisfaction if he will put an end to his anger. Let him relent! Only Hades is so unrelenting and unyielding, which is why he is the most hated by mortals of all the gods.

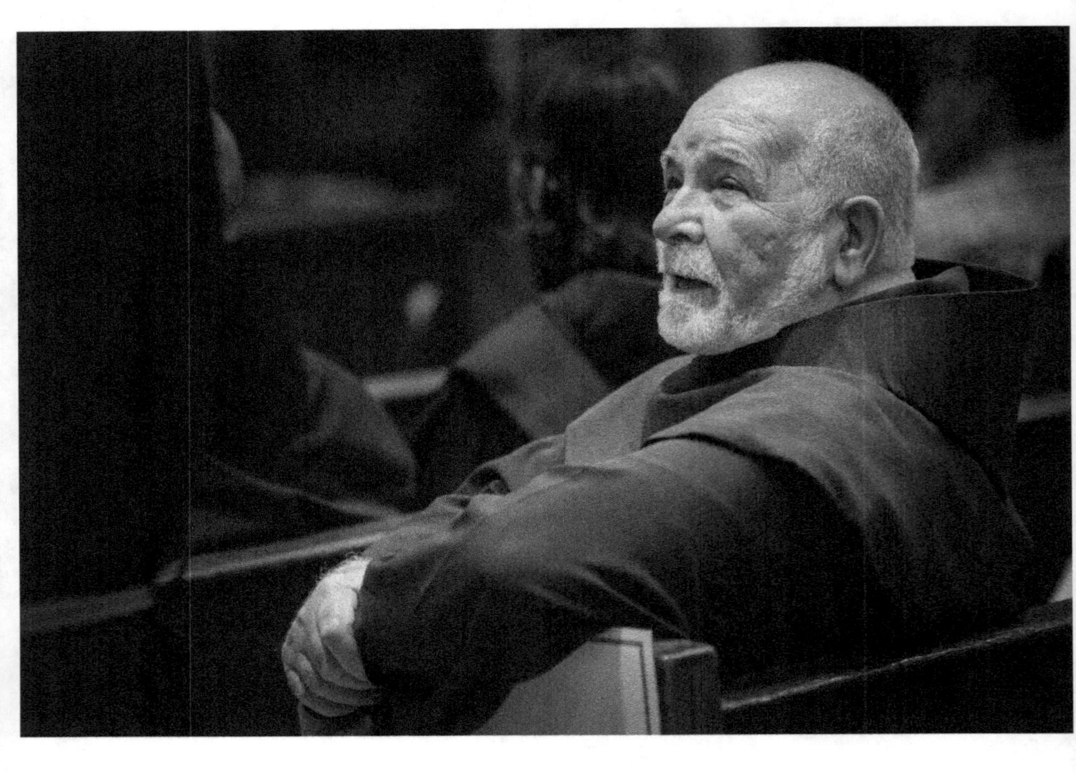

44

Nestor, the wise elder. Elder, yes, but he stands on the battlefield, engaged in the combat.

We, who have not seen combat, sit with our sage, elder, bearded poetry professor who has bound his edition of the *Iliad* in board and leather. The glue is still stuck to his hands, which are stained with ink from stamping an Ex Libris on the frontispiece. We eat cheeseburgers and discuss the gods at the Chelsea Gallery diner on Seventh Avenue.

Nestor addresses Achilles with a rousing speech and recounts a glorious past to counter the downcast malaise of the moment.

εἴθ' ὣς ἡβώοιμι βίη δέ μοι ἔμπεδος εἴη
ὡς ὁπότ' Ἠλείοισι καὶ ἡμῖν νεῖκος ἐτύχθη

If only I were young again, if only my strength were steadfast in my limbs, as when the Elean clash began . . .

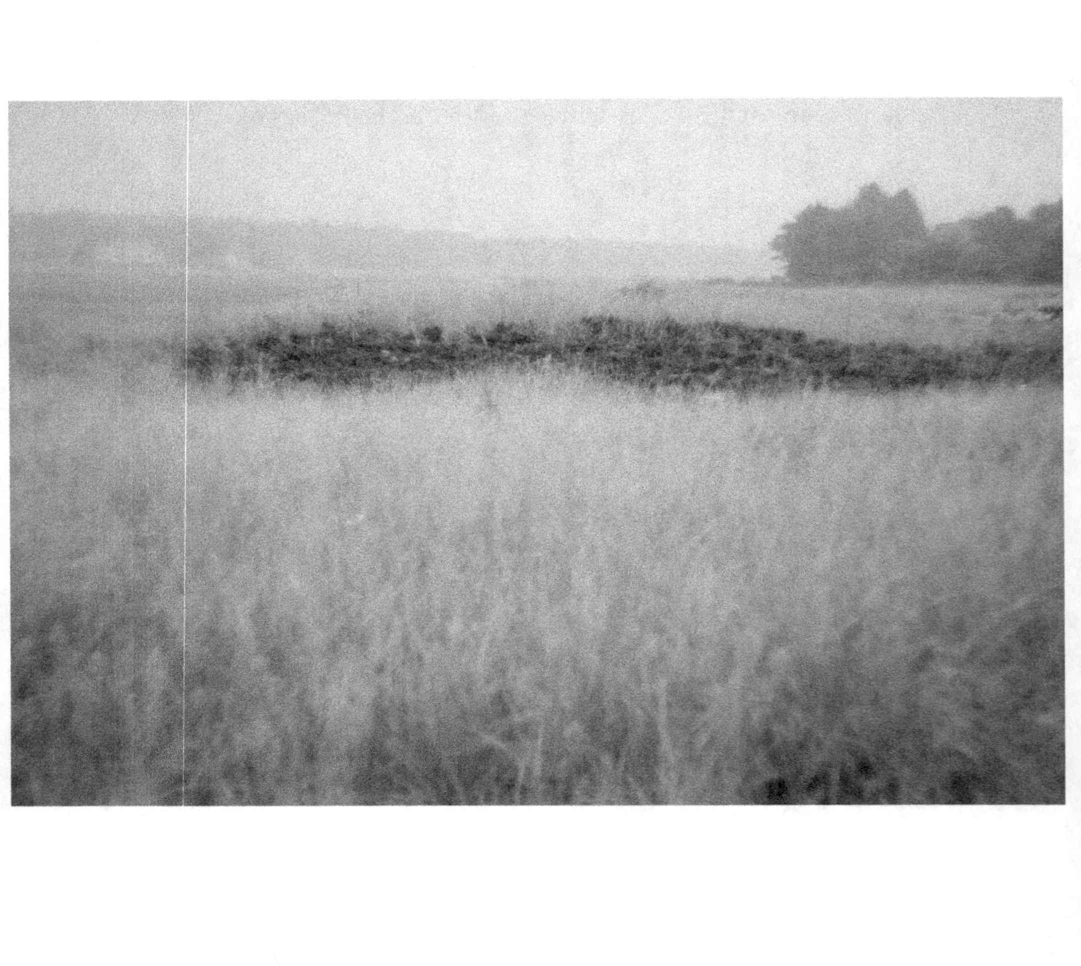

43

The gods step on the earth to raise the stakes.

They are not disinterested parties, but take an active role in the action. They are agents of fate. Hera asks Zeus for help. Zeus tells her to take Athena with her to the plains of Troy to spur on the Argives. Athena herself is a weapon.

With golden-winged stallions, Hera descends to make sure the killing does not stop.

ἀλλ' ὅτε δὴ Τροίην ἷξον ποταμώ τε ῥέοντε,
ἧχι ῥοὰς Σιμόεις συμβάλλετον ἠδὲ Σκάμανδρος,
ἔνθ' ἵππους ἔστησε θεὰ λευκώλενος Ἥρη
λύσασ' ἐξ ὀχέων, περὶ δ' ἠέρα πουλὺν ἔχευε:

But when they arrived at Troy, with its two flowing rivers,
where Simois and Scamander combine their streams, there
Hera, the white-armed goddess, reined her horses, unhitched
them from the chariot, and surrounded them in concealing mist.

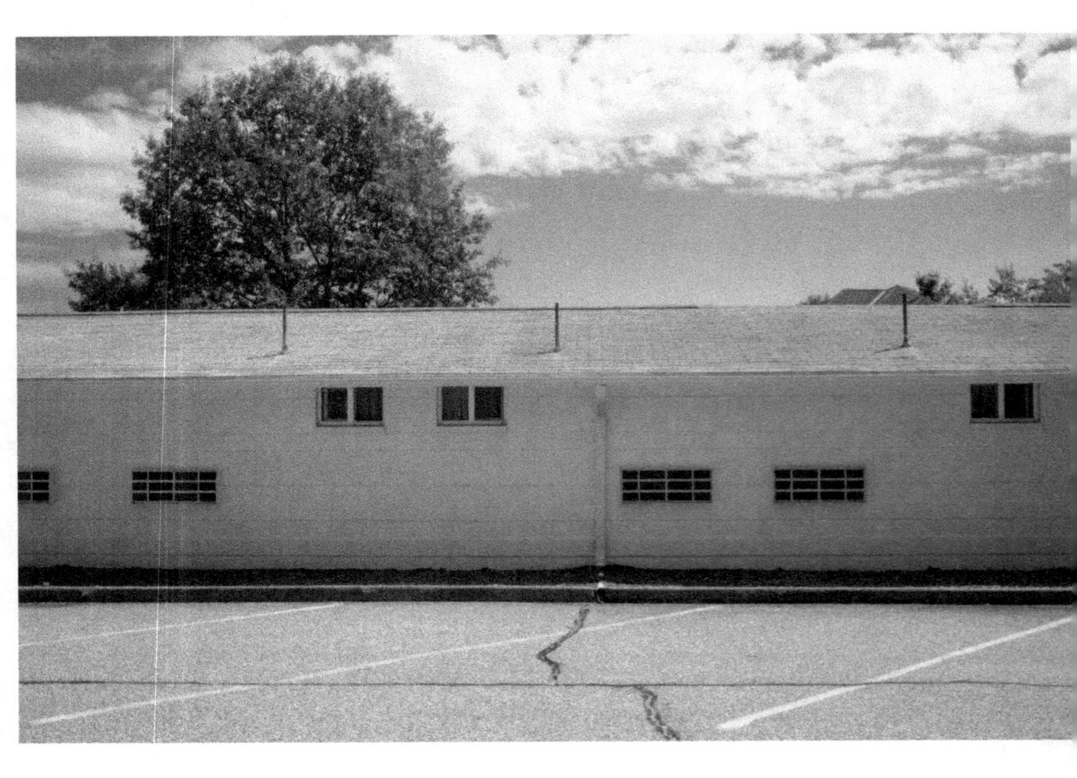

42

Maybe you have heard the phrase "rosy-fingered dawn"? It is a favorite of Homer's.

ῥοδοδάκτυλος Ἠώς" (rhododaktulos Ēōs).

Just a poetic line and a metaphorical flourish? But the dawn is alive, in the person of a goddess.

The cosmos is filled with people. Sometimes the only difference that seems to matter is that some never die and some do. Otherwise, just people, sharing light.

ἠὼς δ' ἐκ λεχέων παρ' ἀγαυοῦ Τιθωνοῖο
ὄρνυθ', ἵν' ἀθανάτοισι φόως φέροι ἠδὲ βροτοῖσι:

And Dawn rose out of bed from beside noble Tithonus,
so to bring light to both the deathless and the dying ones.

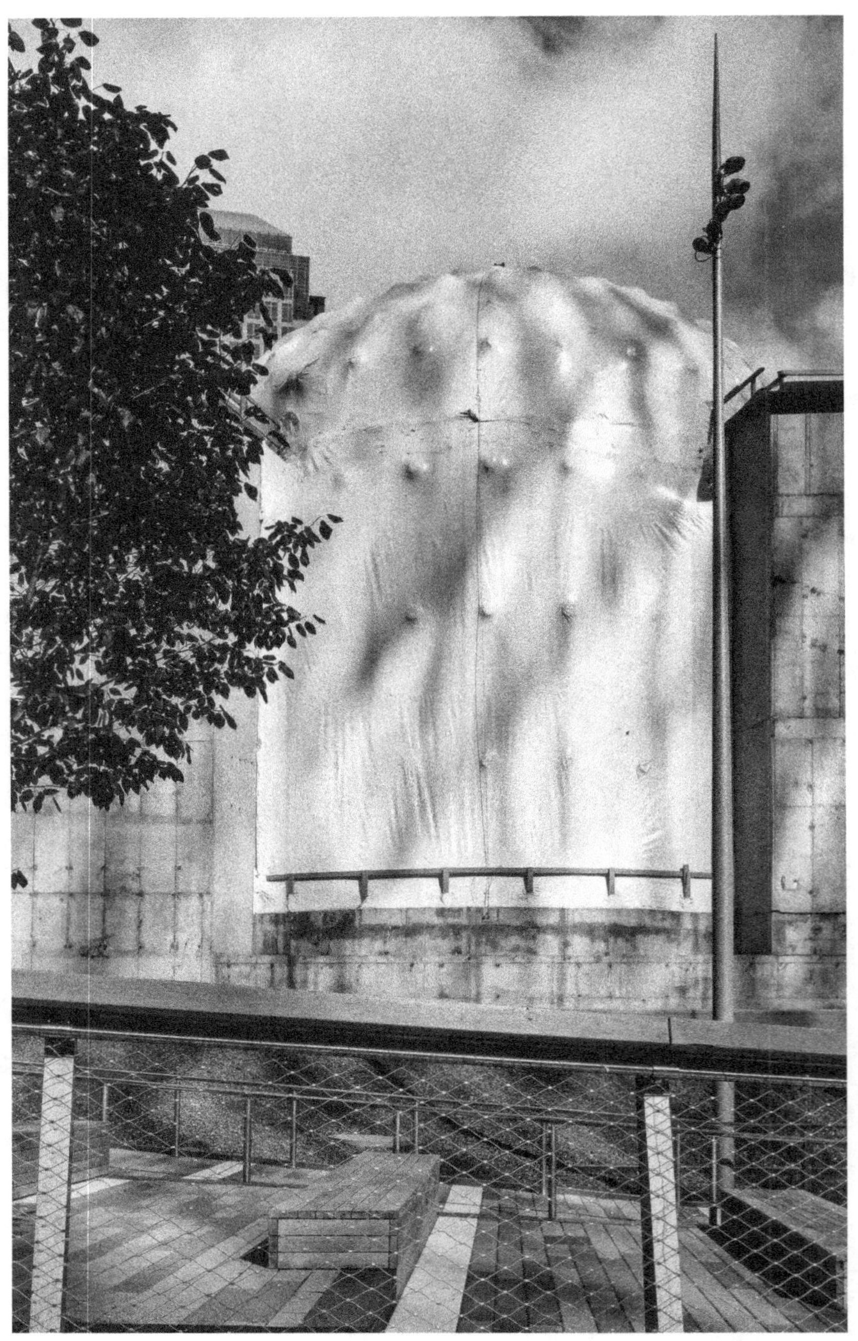

41

Do not forget Poseidon and his grudge against Troy.

He was never paid as promised for building those walls. Do not forget that Poseidon is an Olympian, that he leaves the sea and sits on mountaintops to view the combatants.

That the ground shakes beneath his feet. That he is a shape-shifter and takes the form of the prophet Calchas. That his speech spurs the two warriors, both named Ajax, to beat back Hector's sortie from behind the walls to the Argive ships.

οὐδ᾽ ἀλαοσκοπιὴν εἶχε κρείων ἐνοσίχθων·
καὶ γὰρ ὃ θαυμάζων ἧστο πτόλεμόν τε μάχην τε
ὑψοῦ ἐπ᾽ ἀκροτάτης κορυφῆς Σάμου ὑληέσσης
Θρηϊκίης· ἔνθεν γὰρ ἐφαίνετο πᾶσα μὲν Ἴδη,
φαίνετο δὲ Πριάμοιο πόλις καὶ νῆες Ἀχαιῶν.

But the mighty Earthshaker was no blind watcher.
He sat, marveling at the warscape, surveying each battle
from the top of the highest peak of forested Samothrace.
Before him spread the whole expanse of Ida; visible too,
lay Priam's city and the vast fleet of Achaean ships.

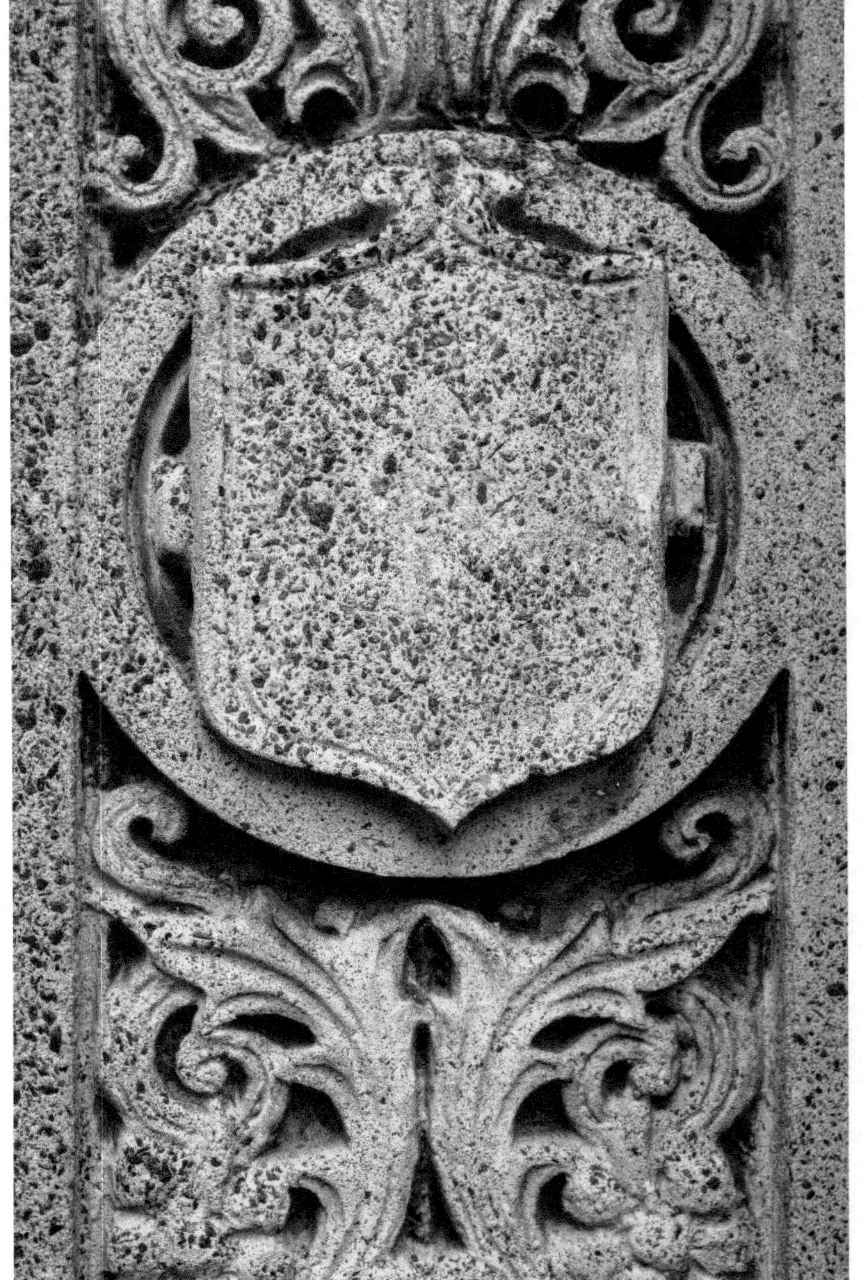

40

Achilles watches Patroclus, in tears, approach.

Achilles tells him that he resembles a baby girl looking to be picked up and hugged. Patroclus replies with a prayer that he never suffers such intractable rage as Achilles. And then he asks, he pleads, to be allowed to fight disguised in Achilles' armor. That the very sight of what appears to be Achilles returning to battle will turn the tides.

This request conjures the image of the great armor, the helmet gleaming, approaching the walls of Troy. Daydreams of Trojans fleeing before a mere reflection.

Sunlight on steel, with the boy inside the breastplate.

μὴ ἐμέ γ᾽ οὖν οὗτός γε λάβοι χόλος, ὃν σὺ φυλάσσεις
αἰναρέτη: τί σευ ἄλλος ὀνήσεται ὀψίγονός περ
αἴ κε μὴ Ἀργείοισιν ἀεικέα λοιγὸν ἀμύνῃς;

Never, I pray, may I harbor such anger as seethes within you. Best in brutality, what good can you do for anyone — even of generations yet to be born, unless you beat back this disgraceful disaster for the Argives?

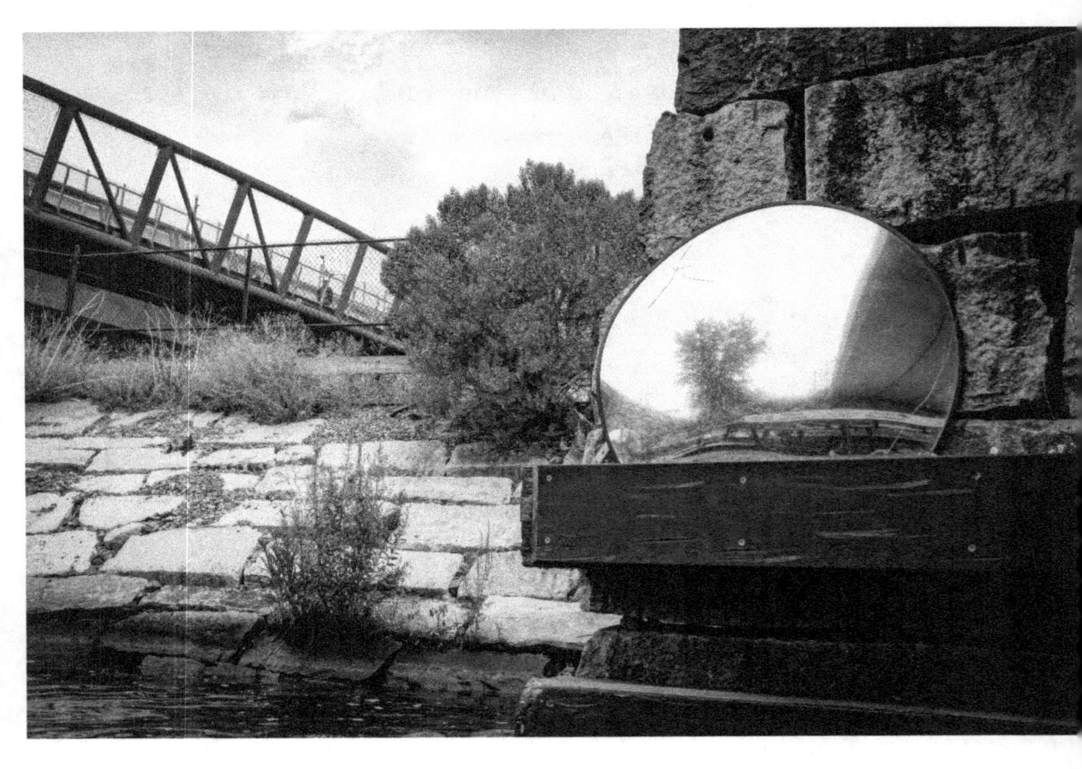

39

There is a limit.

It is not set by the mortal human cohorts. It is not set by the Olympians. It is set by the rivers.

Before Hector dies, Achilles fights the river Xanthus. Xanthus, choked by the bodies and blood of Achilles' slaughter, cries to his brother river, the Simois. Even if there is no limit to the carnage, there is a limit when a mortal sustains an attack on an immortal.

οὐδὲ Σκάμανδρος ἔληγε τὸ ὃν μένος, ἀλλ᾽ ἔτι μᾶλλον
χώετο Πηλεΐωνι, κόρυσσε δὲ κῦμα ῥόοιο
ὑψόσ᾽ ἀειρόμενος, Σιμόεντι δὲ κέκλετ᾽ ἀΰσας:
φίλε κασίγνητε σθένος ἀνέρος ἀμφότεροί περ

But Scamander would not relent in his rage against Achilles, and in fury he raised up a massive surging wave, and lifting its crest, he bellowed to Simois — "My brother, together we must meet this man's force with our flood . . .

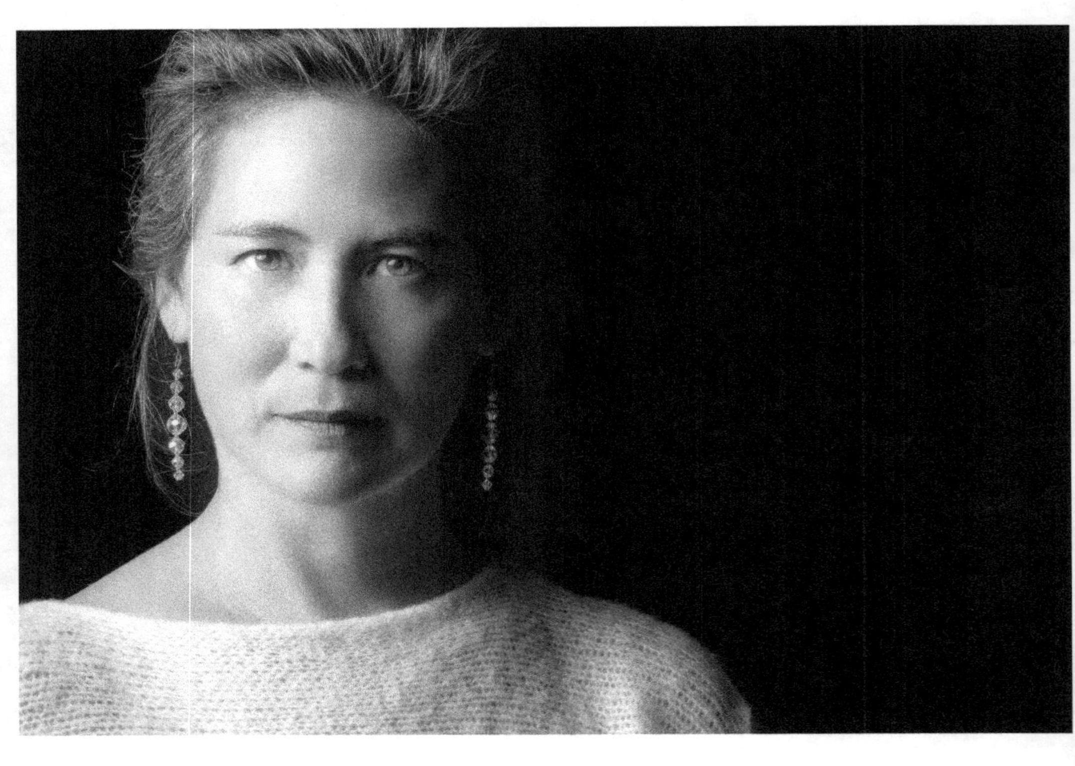

38

She did everything right.

Just as Hector asked. To pray, to plead, to make sacrifice to Athena to stop Diomedes and break his spear. The great queen pulled the most beautiful, brocaded, scented Sidonian robe from the storeroom. She brought it to Theano, the chosen priestess of Athena, to lay over the knees of the statue in supplication.

She did everything right. But Athena refused the offering.

τῶν ἕν' ἀειραμένη Ἑκάβη φέρε δῶρον Ἀθήνῃ,
ὃς κάλλιστος ἔην ποικίλμασιν ἠδὲ μέγιστος,
ἀστὴρ δ' ὣς ἀπέλαμπεν: ἔκειτο δὲ νείατος ἄλλων.

Hecuba lifted up the robe, the one to offer Athena,
the most beautifully embroidered and the largest,
the one that shone like a star, stowed beneath all the others.

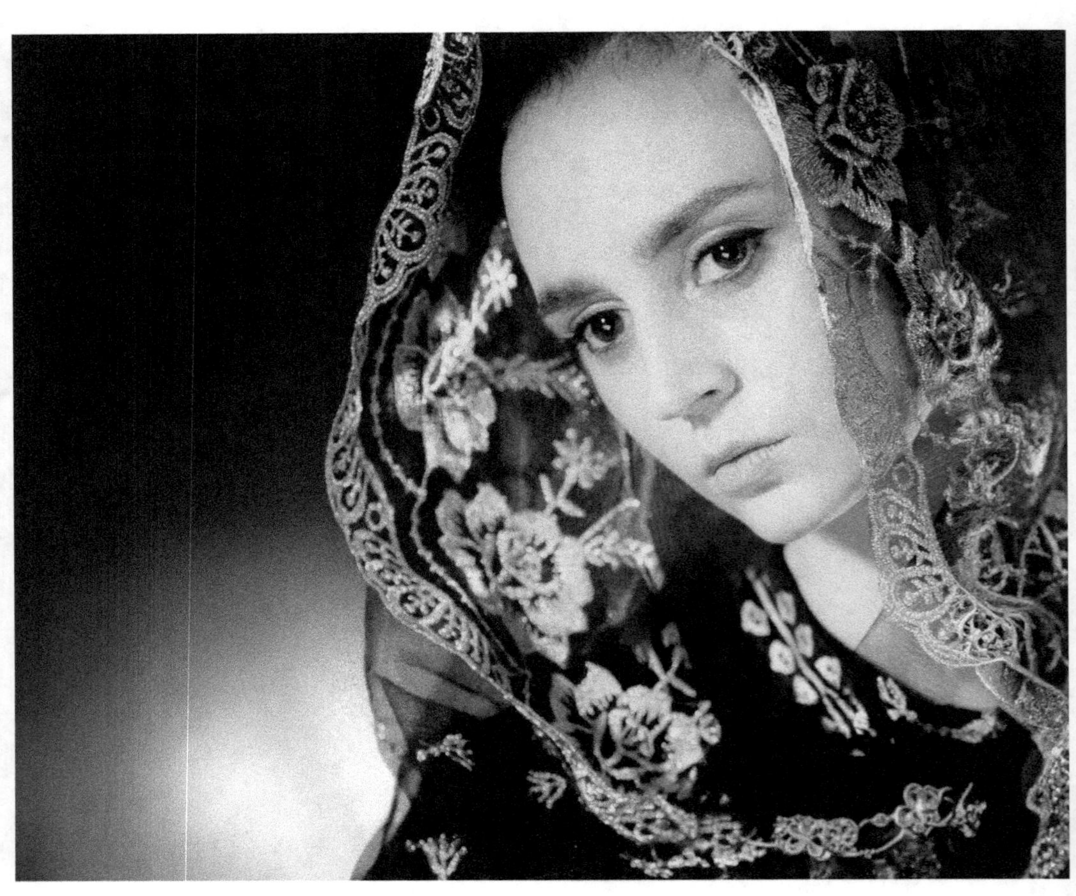

37

There are two women named Laodice. One is a daughter of Agamemnon. The other, a daughter of Priam and Hecuba.

Laodice of Troy is so lovely, the goddess Iris impersonates her when appearing to Helen. Homer describes her as "the loveliest daughter Hecuba ever bred" as she accompanies the queen to meet Hector. That is all we ever hear of her.

We do not ever meet Agamemnon's Laodice. She is one of his three daughters, along with Chrysothemis and Iphianassa, offered to Achilles as a bribe for him to return to the battlefield. We hear her name when Agamemnon announces the offer and once again when Odysseus relays the offer to Achilles. She must be lovely, too.

Ἶρις δ’ αὖθ’ Ἑλένῃ λευκωλένῳ ἄγγελος ἦλθεν
εἰδομένη γαλόῳ Ἀντηνορίδαο δάμαρτι,
τὴν Ἀντηνορίδης εἶχε κρείων Ἑλικάων
Λαοδίκην Πριάμοιο θυγατρῶν εἶδος ἀρίστην.

Iris went up to white-armed Helen as a messenger, putting on the likeness of her sister-in-law — the wife of Antenor's son, Helicaon's bride — Laodice, the most beautiful to behold of Priam's daughters.

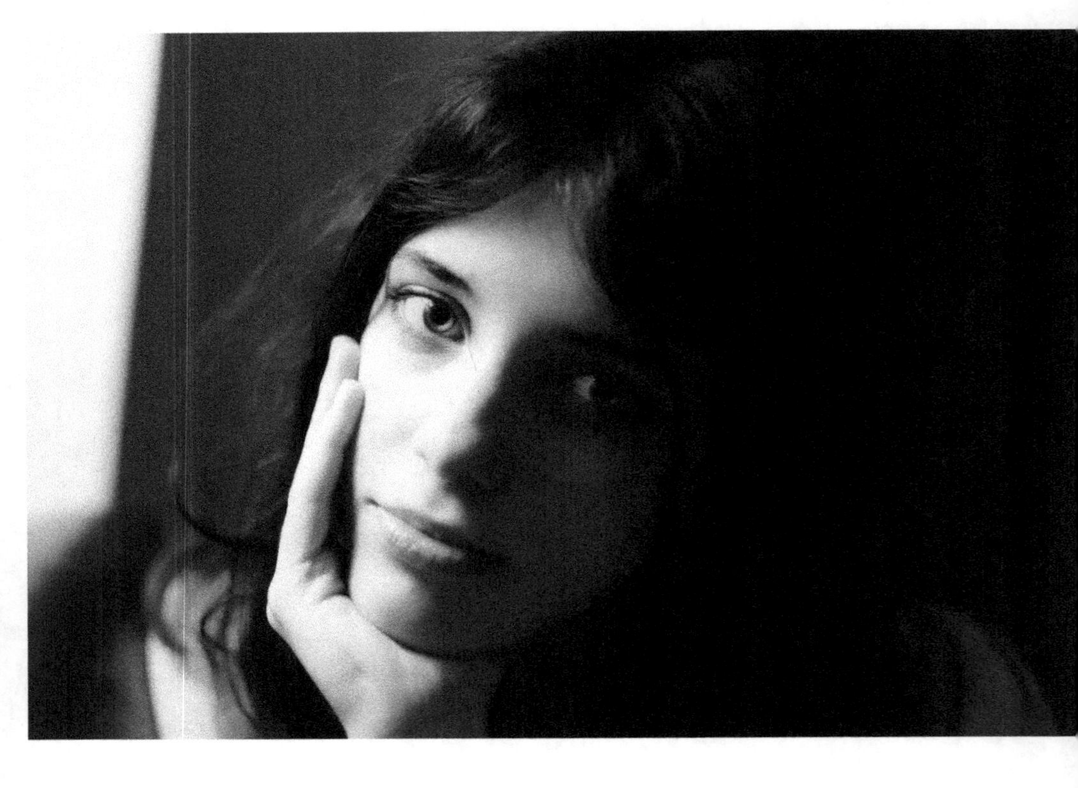

36

Sometimes the fierce gods heal.

Aeneas was wounded by Diomedes. Apollo swept him off the battlefield and placed him within the sacred citadel of Pergamus. There, within Apollo's own temple. But it wasn't Apollo who healed him.

Apollo's mother and sister minister to the Trojan mortal who will go on, once Virgil appropriates him, to found the Roman race. So Augustus can command a history as glorious as the Greek's.

ἤτοι τὸν Λητώ τε καὶ Ἄρτεμις ἰοχέαιρα
ἐν μεγάλῳ ἀδύτῳ ἀκέοντό τε κύδαινόν τε:

There, Leta and Artemis the shooter of arrows,
in the holy of holies of the great inner shrine,
healed him and brought him great glory.

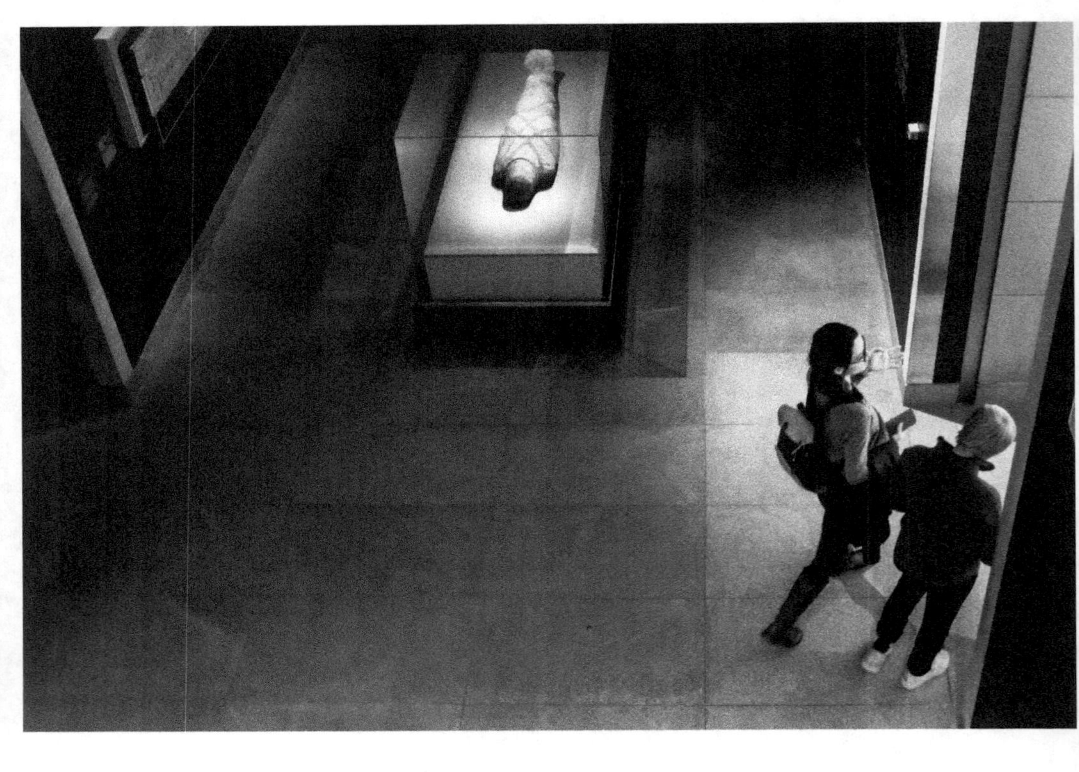

35

It took a great imagining.

Homer portrays the intimate details of a world that preceded him by about four hundred years. Hector, Achilles, Agamemnon, Helen were as distant from Homer as Shakespeare, Elizabeth I, James I, and Robert Dudley, first earl of Leicester, are distant from us.

We owe it all to the singers. Immortality belongs to the singers.

ὣς ἔφαθ', οἳ δὲ διέστησαν καὶ εἶξαν ἀπήνῃ.
οἳ δ' ἐπεὶ εἰσάγαγον κλυτὰ δώματα, τὸν μὲν ἔπειτα
τρητοῖς ἐν λεχέεσσι θέσαν, παρὰ δ' εἶσαν ἀοιδοὺς

So he spoke, and the people gathered stepped aside to make way for the cart to pass. And when they carried him into the famed halls, they laid him out on a carven bed, and beside him, the leaders of song raised the chanted dirge.

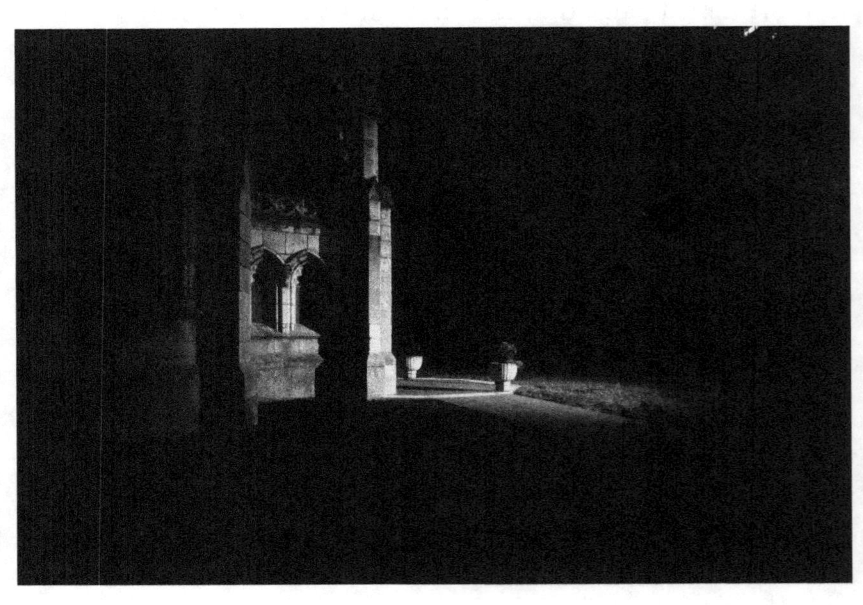

34

Well before dawn, Nestor shouts beside the tent of Odysseus to wake him. The sound careens off the ships' timber and startles the great tactician from sleep.

Sleep and wine were the only soothing gifts from the gods. But now was a time for rousing a mission to infiltrate the Trojan ranks in darkness.

‘τίς δ᾽ οὗτος κατὰ νῆας ἀνὰ στρατὸν ἔρχεαι οἶος
νύκτα δι᾽ ὀρφναίην, ὅτε θ᾽ εὕδουσι βροτοὶ ἄλλοι,
ἠέ τιν᾽ οὐρήων διζήμενος, ἤ τιν᾽ ἑταίρων;
φθέγγεο, μηδ᾽ ἀκέων ἐπ᾽ ἔμ᾽ ἔρχεο: τίπτε δέ σε χρεώ;

Who are you, wandering amid the ships in the dark of night,
alone, when other mortals are sleeping soundlessly?
Are you seeking out a mule-guard or a comrade?
Speak up — stop this silent creeping. What's driving you?

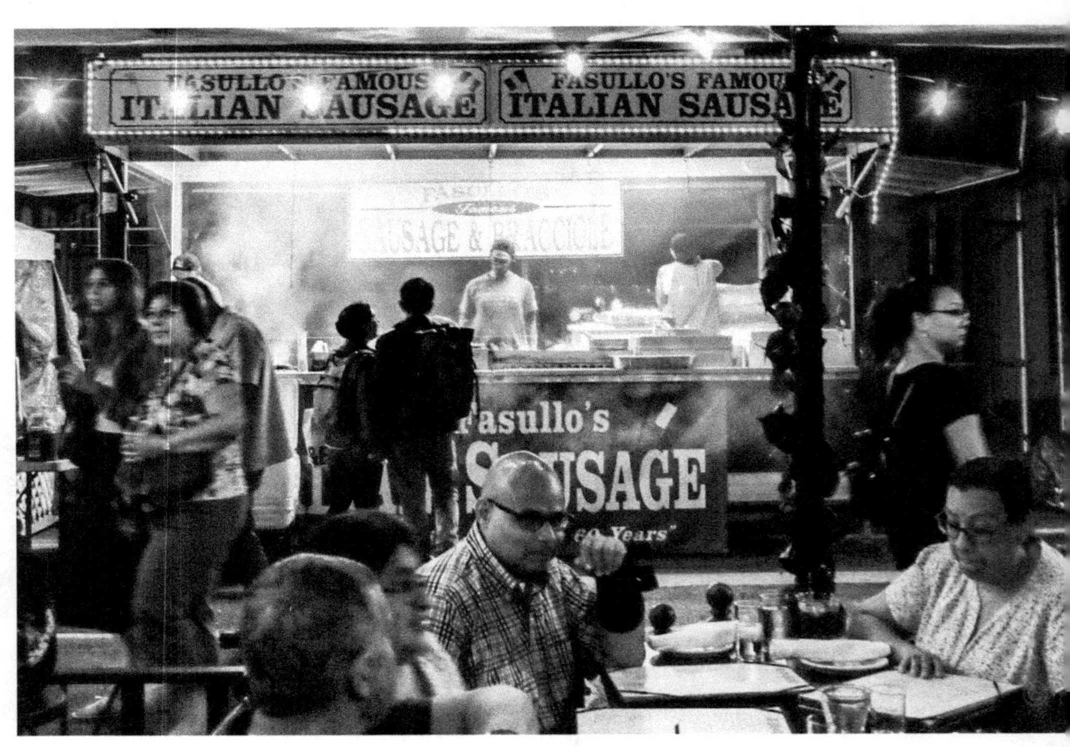
FASULLO'S FAMOU
ITALIAN SAUSA E
Fasullo's
SAUSAGE

33

Sacrifice fulfills.

The feasts follow the fighting with ritual worship of the gods. When the duels between the heroes conclude, the feasting begins. After Ajax and Hector part, still very much alive, the war subsides for the moment.

Both sides welcome their warrior's return, and the smoke rises to satisfy the deathless deities.

μίστυλλόν τ' ἄρα τἆλλα καὶ ἀμφ' ὀβελοῖσιν ἔπειραν,
ὤπτησάν τε περιφραδέως, ἐρύσαντό τε πάντα.
αὐτὰρ ἐπεὶ παύσαντο πόνου τετύκοντό τε δαῖτα
δαίνυντ', οὐδέ τι θυμὸς ἐδεύετο δαιτὸς ἐΐσης.

They carved the rest of the meat, put the pieces on spits to be turned and roasted, until they took them off the flame and prepared for the feast — their work finished, they spread the banquet, so not one lacked a share to gorge to his heart's content.

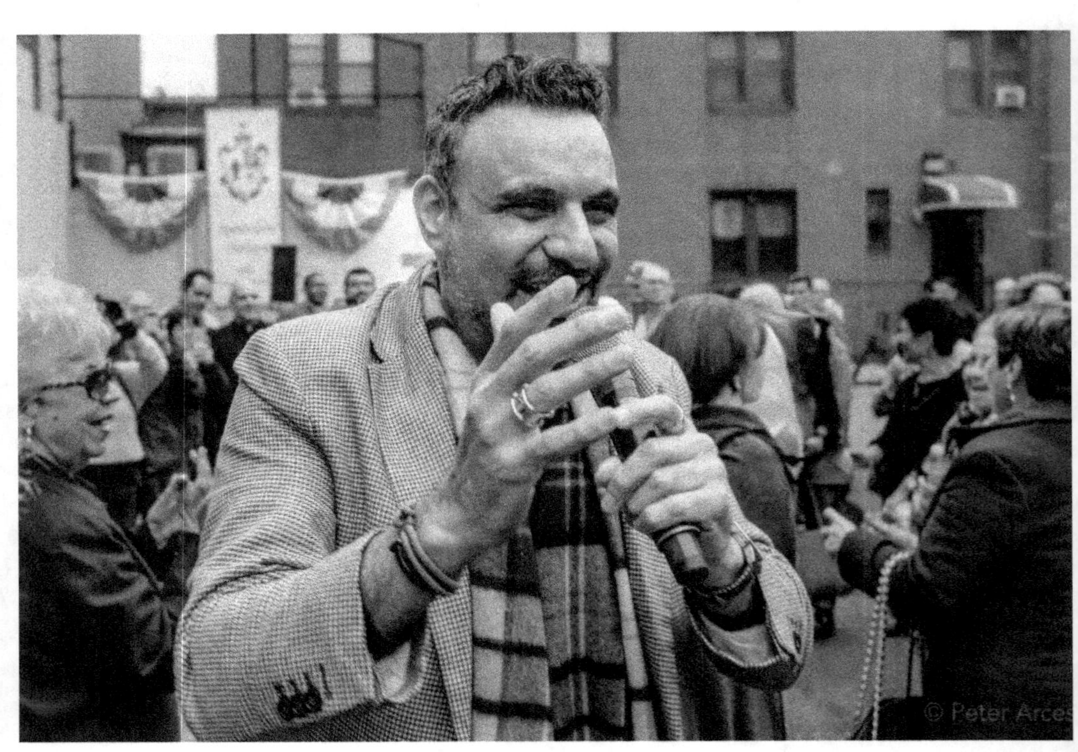

32

Aside from prayerful petitions, dirges, and laments, there is little to no song in the *Iliad.*

Hector, bloody from the battlefield, stands in Helen's bedroom beside his brother. Helen exhorts him to sit beside her and rest. She offers him sympathy and acknowledgment.

Hector refuses but accepts the expression of care. The song remains silent for now.

ἀλλ᾽ ἄγε νῦν εἴσελθε καὶ ἕζεο τῷδ᾽ ἐπὶ δίφρῳ
δᾶερ, ἐπεί σε μάλιστα πόνος φρένας ἀμφιβέβηκεν
εἵνεκ᾽ ἐμεῖο κυνὸς καὶ Ἀλεξάνδρου ἕνεκ᾽ ἄτης,
οἷσιν ἐπὶ Ζεὺς θῆκε κακὸν μόρον, ὡς καὶ ὀπίσσω
ἀνθρώποισι πελώμεθ᾽ ἀοίδιμοι ἐσσομένοισι.

Come here now and sit on this chair, my brother-in-law —
such heartache for you, more than for any other, because of my
bitch-eyed self, and my delusional, mad Alexander. Zeus did this
to us, giving us this deadly fate, so evil that people will
remember us for generations in poetic song.

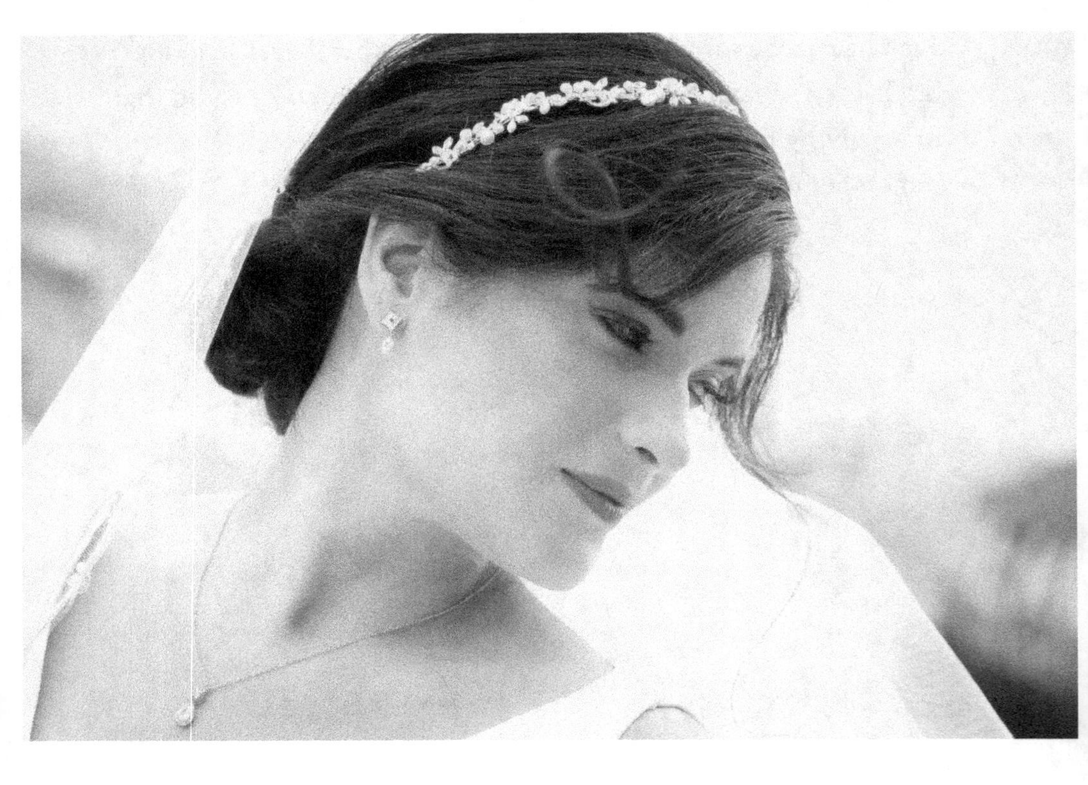

31

The most joyous song is the wedding song.

As with Helen's beauty, you have to imagine. You have to gaze at the silent wonder of Achilles' shield. The new one, forged by Hephaestus to replace the one Patroclus died with, fighting.

You have to look over the shoulder of Thetis as she admires the scene wrought in the metal by the smith god.

ἐν τῇ μέν ῥα γάμοι τ᾽ ἔσαν εἰλαπίναι τε,
νύμφας δ᾽ ἐκ θαλάμων δαΐδων ὕπο λαμπομενάων
ἠγίνεον ἀνὰ ἄστυ, πολὺς δ᾽ ὑμέναιος ὀρώρει:

One shone with weddings and feasts, where a procession of brides under radiant torchlight were led from their rooms through the streets of the city, surrounded by choirs of song.

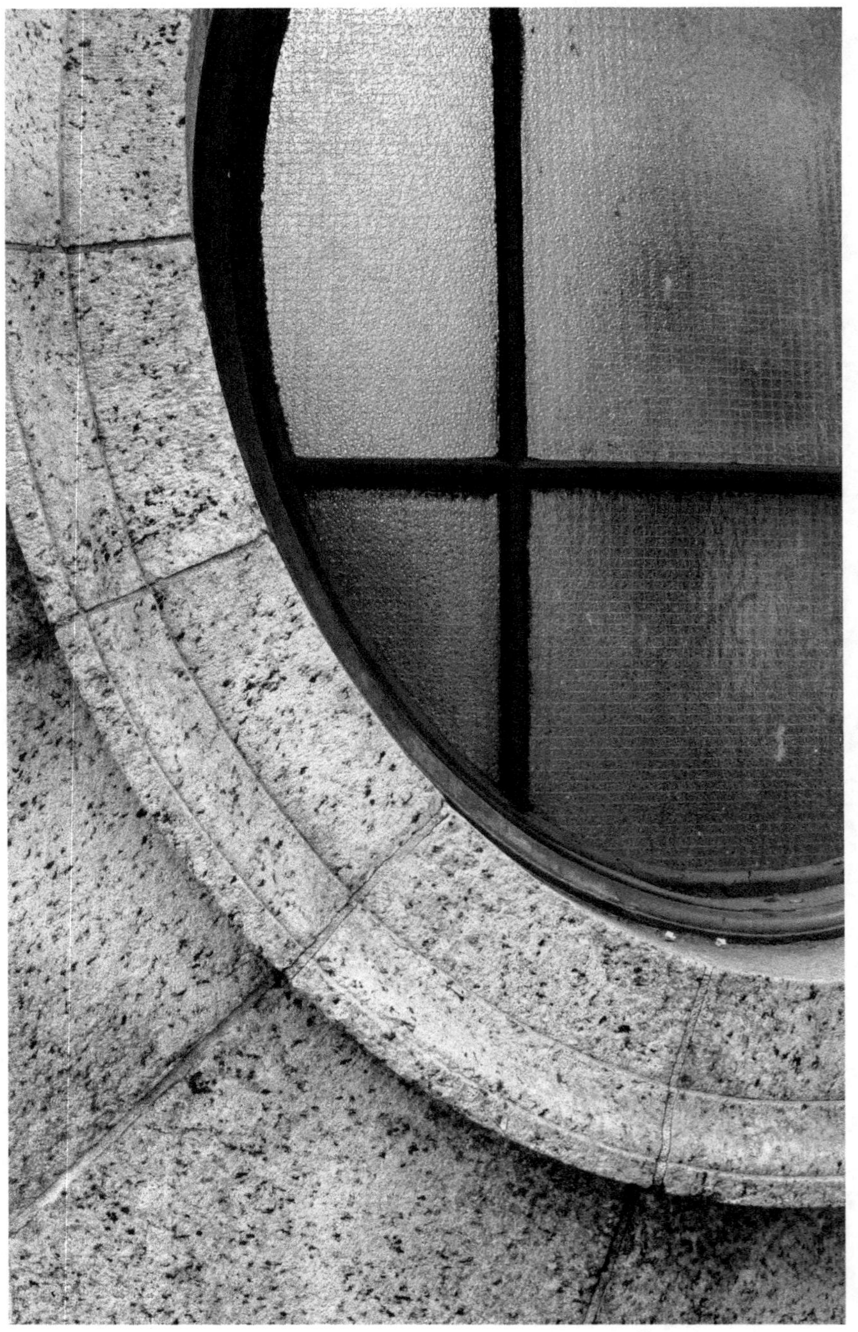

30

The shield of Achilles is a portrait of the world both real and ideal.

Thetis brought the armor to her son. Protection and consolation in the service of vengeance. The cosmos offers more than disillusion.

The cosmos contains more than grievance.

ἐν δ᾽ ἐτίθει ποταμοῖο μέγα σθένος Ὠκεανοῖο
ἄντυγα πὰρ πυμάτην σάκεος πύκα ποιητοῖο.
αὐτὰρ ἐπεὶ δὴ τεῦξε σάκος μέγα τε στιβαρόν τε,
τεῦξ᾽ ἄρα οἱ θώρηκα φαεινότερον πυρὸς αὐγῆς,

All along the rim of the tightly forged shield, he
fashioned the mighty surging river Oceanos.
And once the massive, unshakeable shield was finished,
he forged him a breastplate brighter than blazing flame.

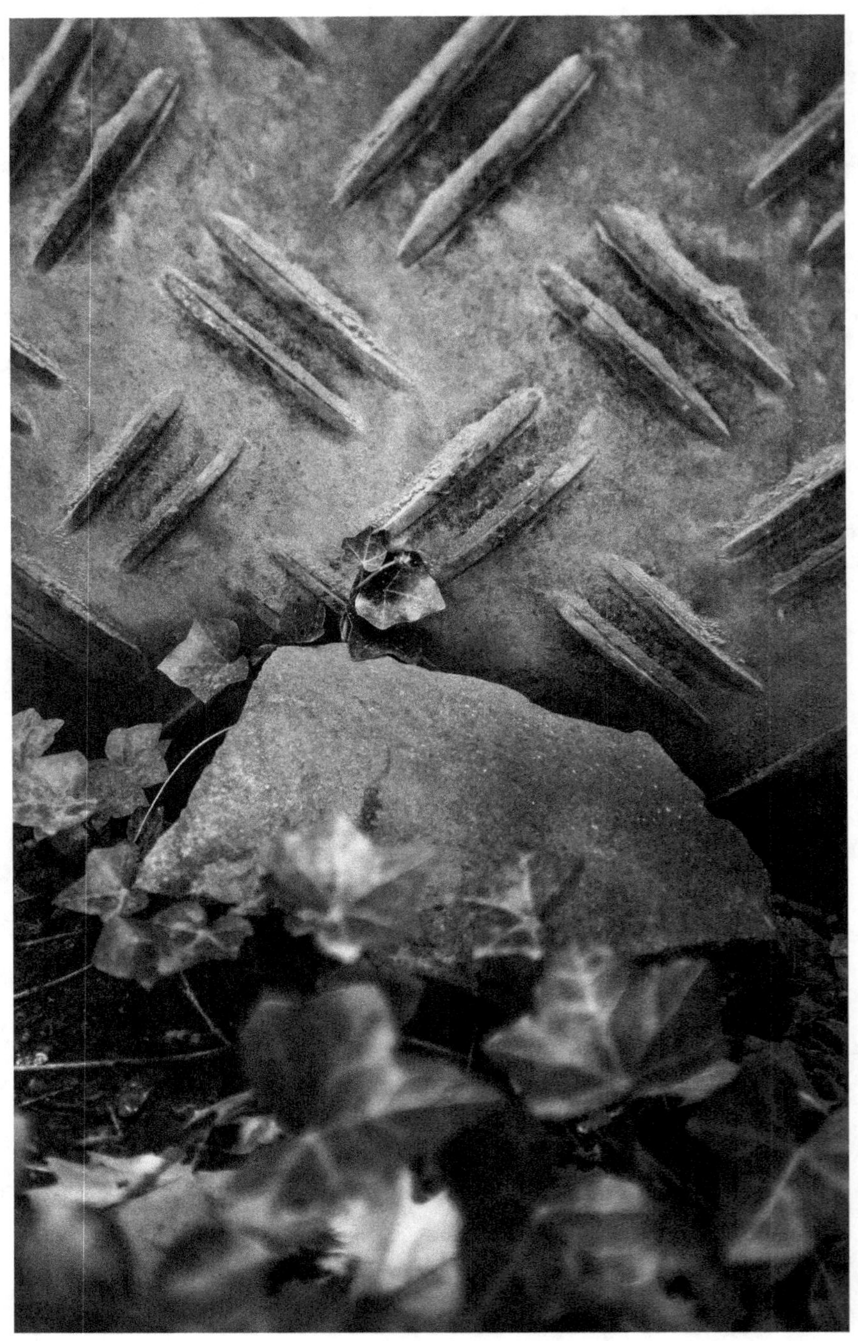

29

"And he forged . . ." repeats each stanza, creating a phantasmagoria of stunning scenes.

Homer does with words what Hephaestus does with fire and bronze. Lift up the shield and you lift up your eyes. It is armor and art, art and armor. Keats made a similar gesture with his Grecian urn.

Auden turned away because he could not bear to see what had become of the world.

ἐν δὲ νομὸν ποίησε περικλυτὸς ἀμφιγυήεις
ἐν καλῇ βήσσῃ μέγαν οἰῶν ἀργεννάων,
σταθμούς τε κλισίας τε κατηρεφέας ἰδὲ σηκούς.

And the famed, struggle-gaited god forged a pasture,
folded into the lush green for the white-flecked flocks to graze,
by the shepherd's shanties, overhangs, and sheepfolds.

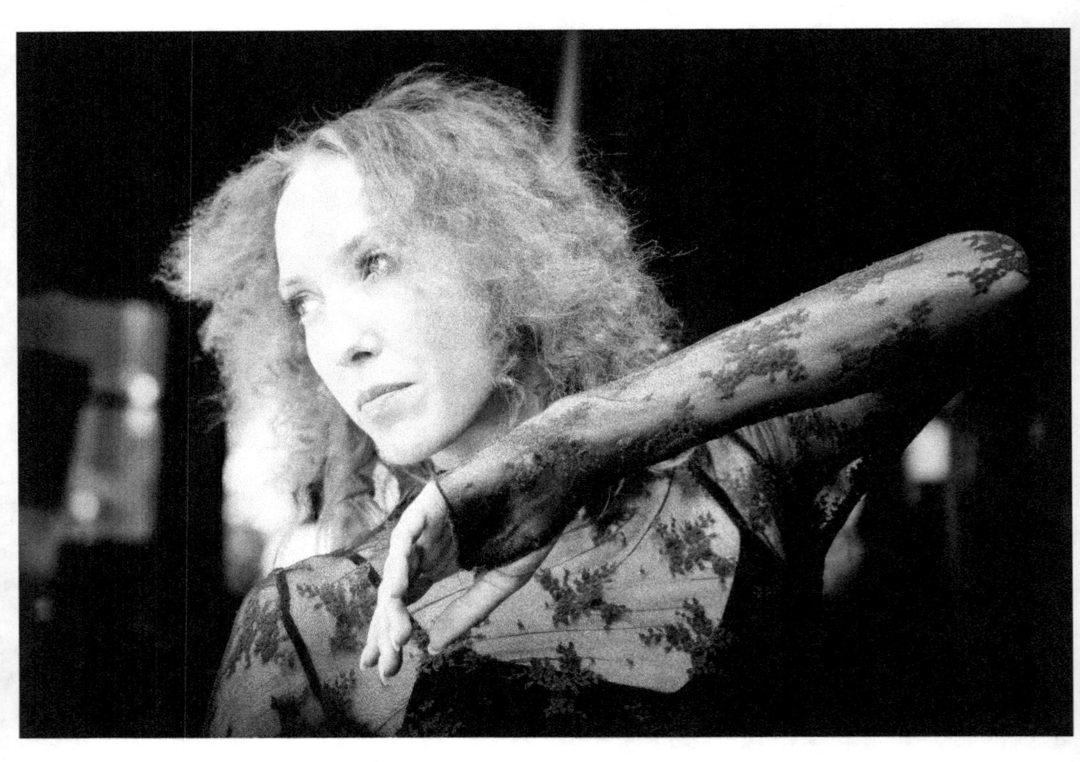

28

The shield sustains a sequence of images.

A series of inspired visions framed in a passage where Homer depicts the world through a set of panels as he pictures it. Was Homer blind? We see nevertheless.

An orchestra for Ariadne.

ἐν δὲ χορὸν ποίκιλλε περικλυτὸς ἀμφιγυήεις,
τῷ ἴκελον οἷόν ποτ᾽ ἐνὶ Κνωσῷ εὐρείῃ
Δαίδαλος ἤσκησεν καλλιπλοκάμῳ Ἀριάδνῃ.

And the famed struggle-gaited god pressed his craft to fashion a dancing place, a circle broad as Daedalus carved onto the vast fields at Knossos — an artful space for Ariadne, the girl with the gleaming curls.

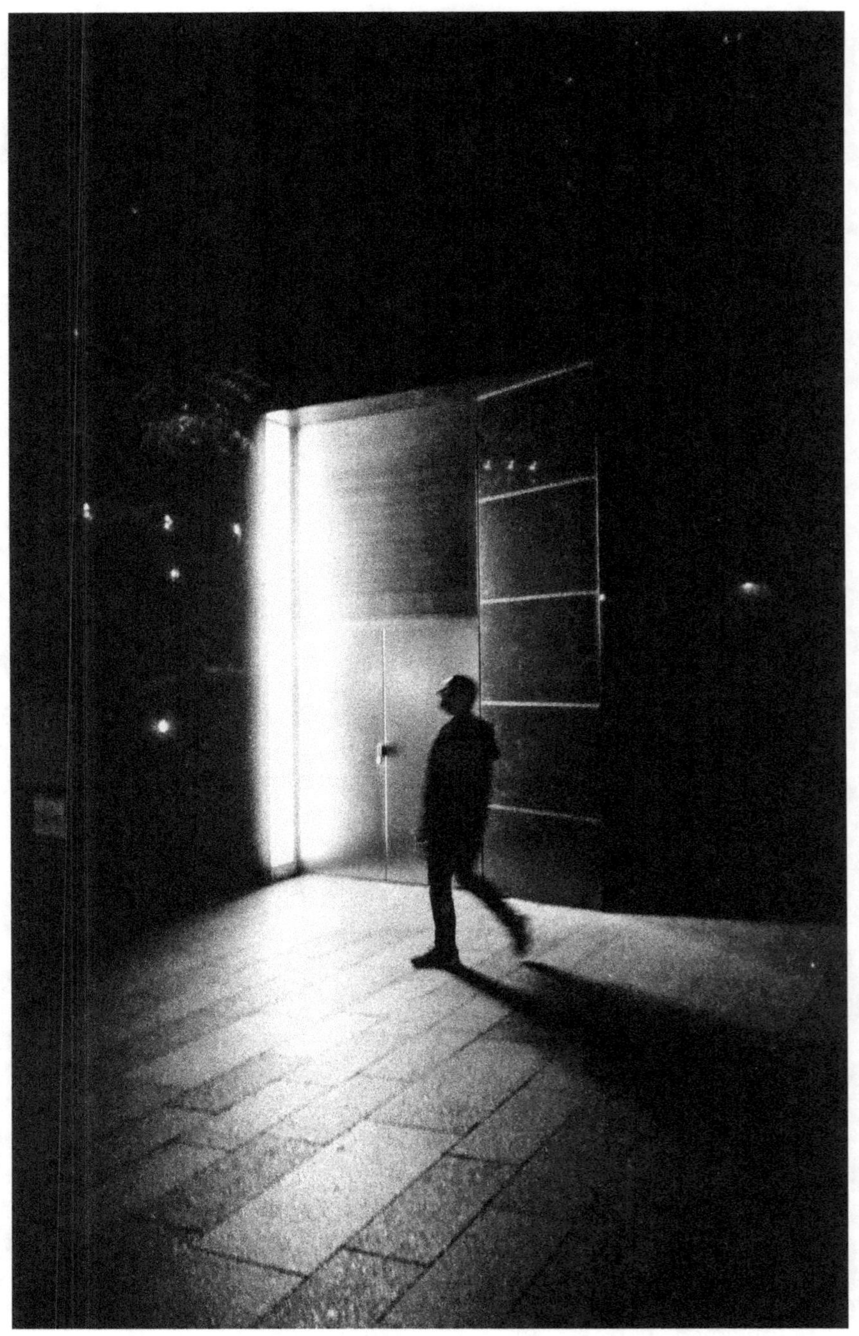

27

The wounded god fashions the shield for the wounded mother of the wounded hero.

The smith's legs broken as an infant thrown from Olympian heights. The grieving heart of the sorrowful mother who knows that her gift indicates the shorter fork of her son's fate.

The warrior who forsakes the love of honor for love.

τοῖσιν δ᾽ ἐν μέσσοισι πάϊς φόρμιγγι λιγείῃ
ἱμερόεν κιθάριζε, λίνον δ᾽ ὑπὸ καλὸν ἄειδε
λεπταλέῃ φωνῇ: τοὶ δὲ ῥήσσοντες ἁμαρτῇ
μολπῇ τ᾽ ἰυγμῷ τε ποσὶ σκαίροντες ἕποντο.

In their midst, a boy played enchantingly on a clear-toned lyre and, with a delicate voice, sang the beautiful Linos dirge while they danced, beating the ground with their feet, in time, shouting and leaping with song.

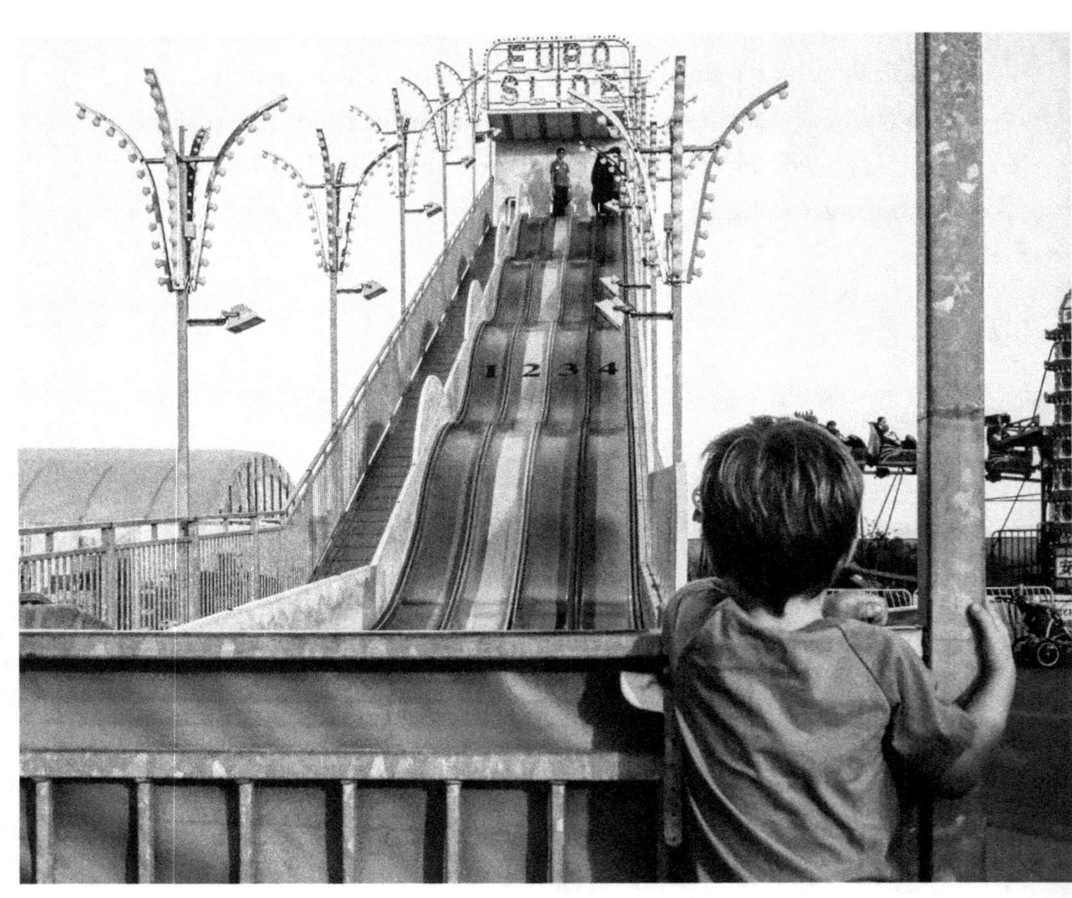
EURO
SLIDE
1 2 3 4

26

Astyanax is derived from two Greek words:

asty (ἄστυ) meaning "city"
anax (ἄναξ) meaning "lord" or "protector"

When combined, the name *Astyanax* can be interpreted as "protector of the city" or "lord of the city."

But my friend insists the name should be rendered "king of the city."

τόν ῥ᾽ Ἕκτωρ καλέεσκε Σκαμάνδριον, αὐτὰρ οἱ ἄλλοι
Ἀστυάνακτ᾽: οἶος γὰρ ἐρύετο Ἴλιον Ἕκτωρ.
ἤτοι ὃ μὲν μείδησεν ἰδὼν ἐς παῖδα σιωπῇ:

Hector always called him Scamandrius, but the others called him Astyanax, the king of the city, because Hector, who was Ilion's sole protection, stood and gazed silently on his son.

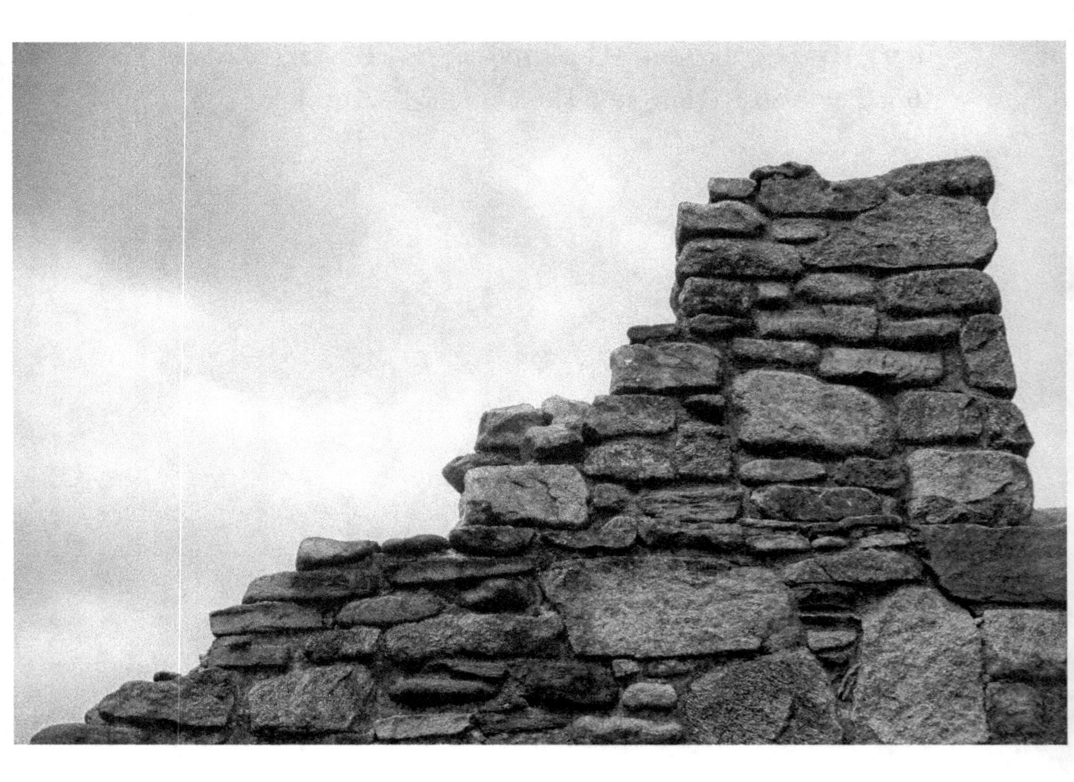

25

She is the woman who did everything right.

She had rushed up to the wall at the Scaean gates. Hector found her at the watchtower. Andromache, the strategist, would have made a good general. She married the right man. Stayed righteously faithful. She gave birth to the right child, to the son promised his father's birthright.

Now, she surveys the field — just in case she can contribute something. Anything to stave off the inevitable.

ἀλλ᾽ ἄγε νῦν ἐλέαιρε καὶ αὐτοῦ μίμν᾽ ἐπὶ πύργῳ,
μὴ παῖδ᾽ ὀρφανικὸν θήῃς χήρην τε γυναῖκα:
λαὸν δὲ στῆσον παρ᾽ ἐρινεόν, ἔνθα μάλιστα
ἀμβατός ἐστι πόλις καὶ ἐπίδρομον ἔπλετο τεῖχος.
τρὶς γὰρ τῇ γ᾽ ἐλθόντες ἐπειρήσανθ᾽ οἱ ἄριστοι
ἀμφ᾽ Αἴαντε δύω καὶ ἀγακλυτὸν Ἰδομενῆα

But come now, stay here on the wall with us — before you make your child an orphan and widow your wife. Station your troops by the wild fig tree — there where the city is most vulnerable, where the walls are lower and more readily scaled. Three times, their best fighters approached that point to test it . . .

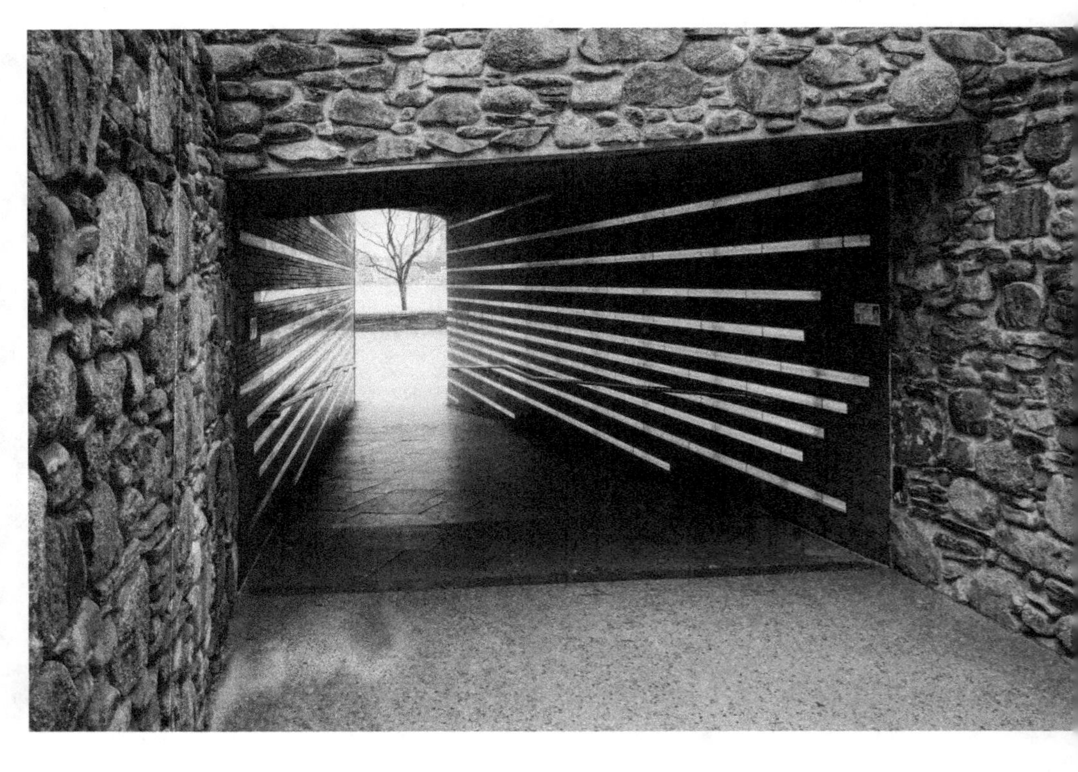

24

Hector knows the fate that will follow him. He will fight anyway. He will fight to avoid shame. He already possesses honor.

Achilles know his fate. He will fight anyway. He will fight out of grief. He will fight for revenge.

At home, Hector confesses.

εὖ γὰρ ἐγὼ τόδε οἶδα κατὰ φρένα καὶ κατὰ θυμόν:
ἔσσεται ἦμαρ ὅτ᾽ ἄν ποτ᾽ ὀλώλῃ Ἴλιος ἱρὴ
καὶ Πρίαμος καὶ λαὸς ἐϋμμελίω Πριάμοιο.

For I know this well in my mind and in my heart:
the day will come when sacred Troy must perish,
along with Priam and Priam's people of the strong
ash spear.

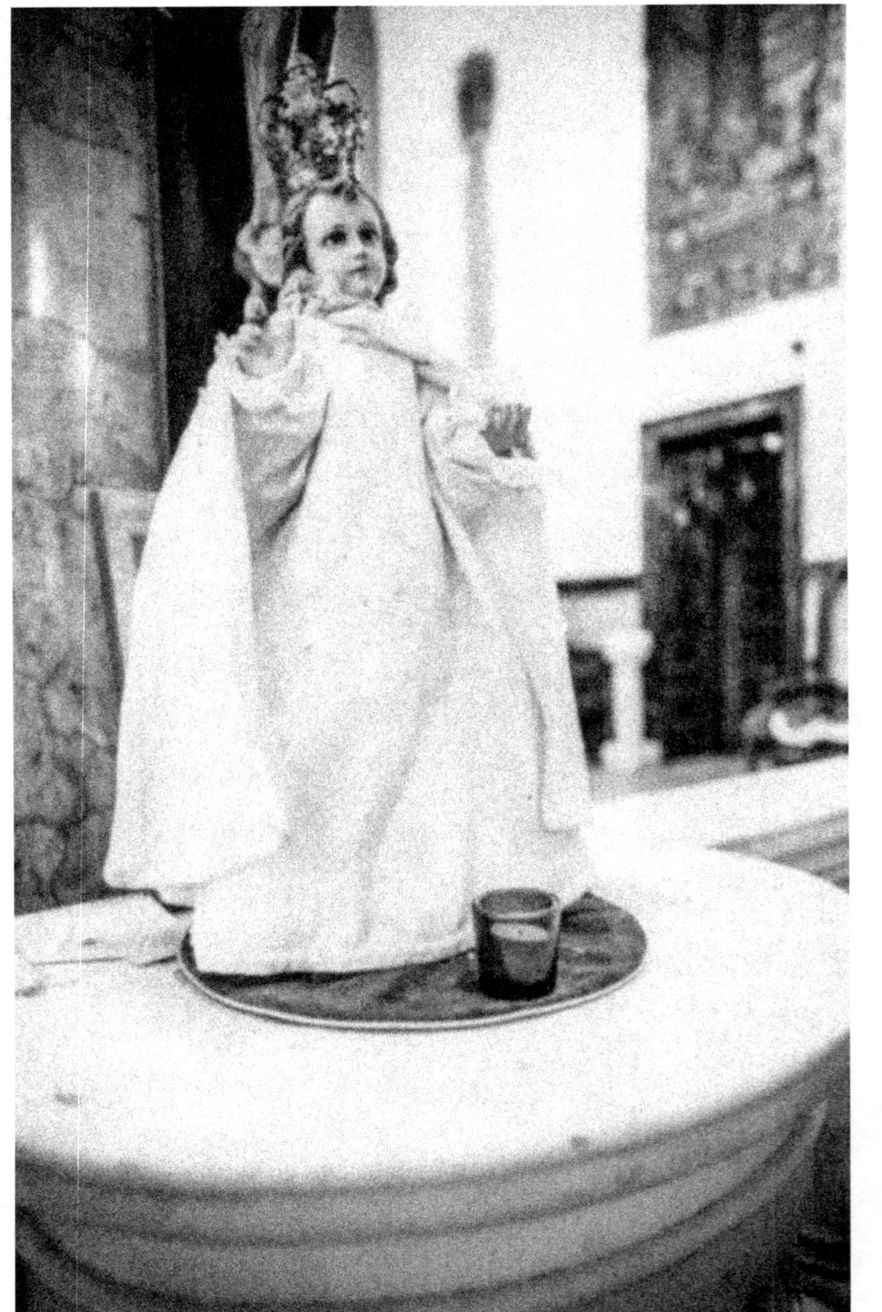

23

Hector reaches out to hold his son. The boy is frightened by the helmet and cries as the sunlight catches the bronze.

The horsehair crest casts a sharp shadow as mother and father lovingly share laughter. Hector removes his helmet and places it on the ground. He raises the child in his arms.

But helmets do not belong on the ground.

αὐτίκ᾽ ἀπὸ κρατὸς κόρυθ᾽ εἵλετο φαίδιμος Ἕκτωρ,
καὶ τὴν μὲν κατέθηκεν ἐπὶ χθονὶ παμφανόωσαν·

Quickly, he lifted the helmet from his head, and glorious Hector placed it on the ground, brightly gleaming.

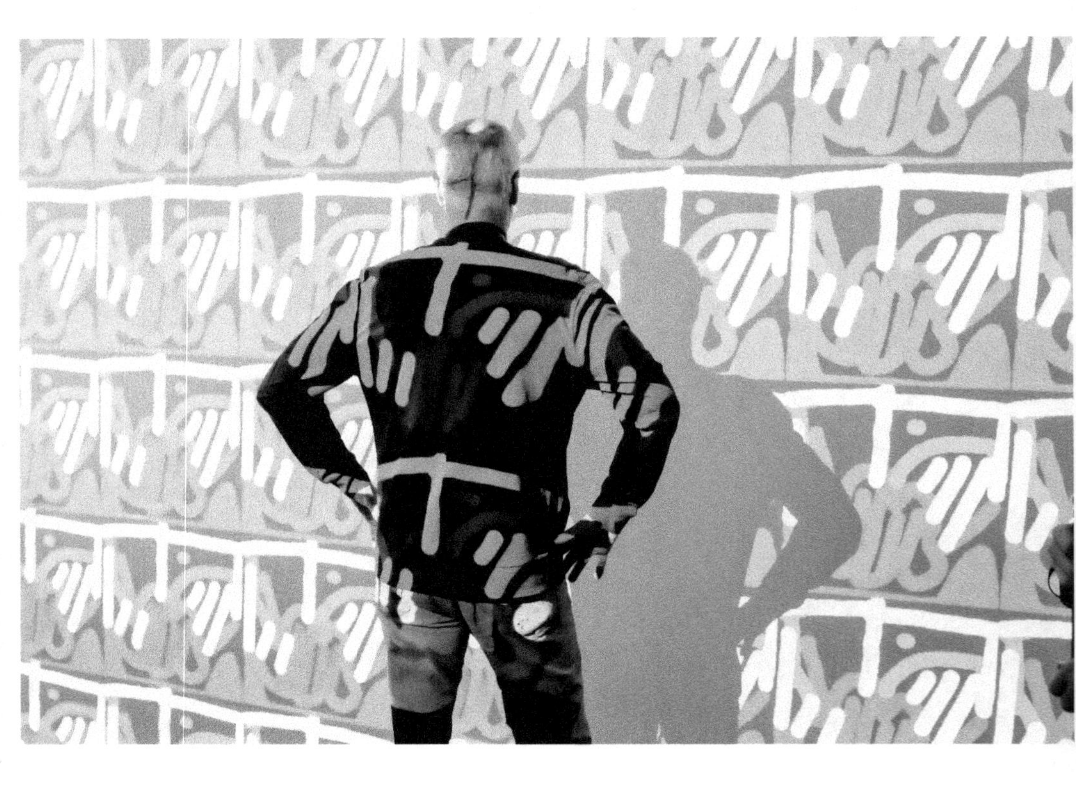

22

About seven centuries later, Publius Vergilius Maro looked back and picked Aeneas to please Augustus.

He needed a founder for the founding myth of Rome. A hero and refugee. A hero who had not killed his brother. A child of Venus, both lover and fighter.

Someone who had stared down the best and lived.

. . . δύο δ᾽ ἀνέρες ἔξοχ᾽ ἄριστοι
ἐς μέσον ἀμφοτέρων συνίτην μεμαῶτε μάχεσθαι
Αἰνείας τ᾽ Ἀγχισιάδης καὶ δῖος Ἀχιλλεύς.

Two warriors — the very best of all — approached
and met between the armies, eager for combat:
Aeneas, son of Anchises, and godly Achilles.

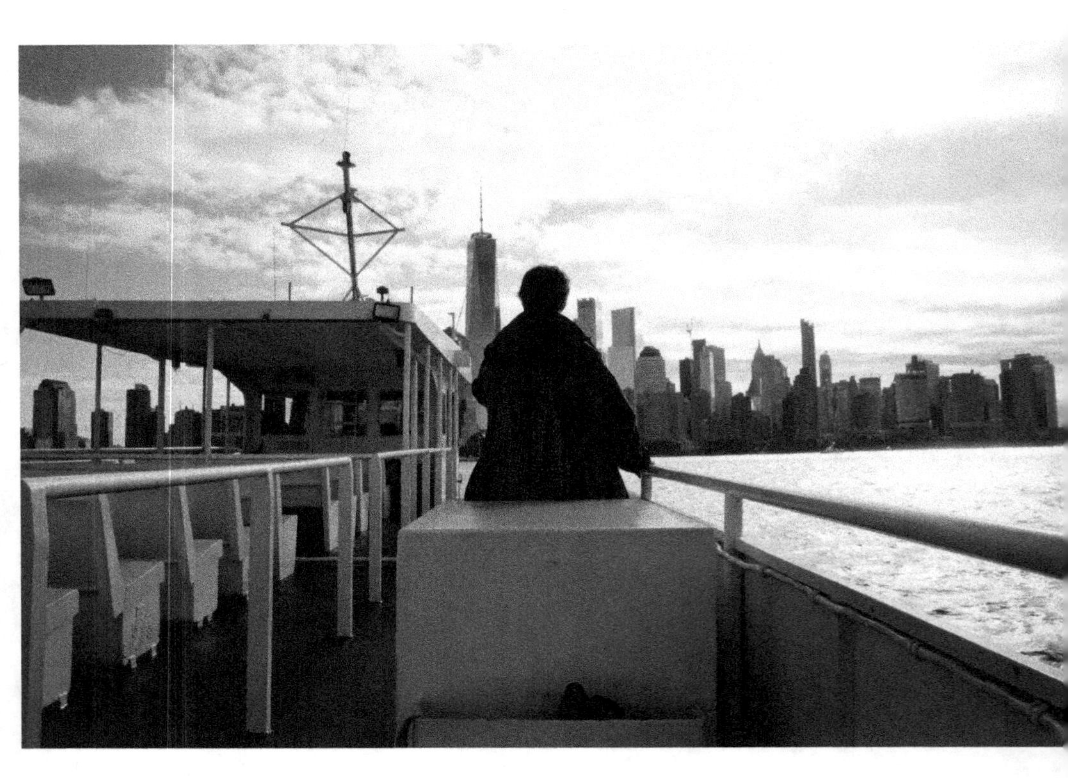

21

Zeus fathered and favored Dardanus. Dardanus founded Dardania. Dardania became Troy. Zeus now strains to sustain his neutrality against the fate of Troy. The transgressions of Troy compound the conundrum.

So when Poseidon, no friend of Troy, advocates for the rescue of Aeneas — why? Why the exception? Is it because Aeneas is a direct descendant of Dardanus? Because he is prophesied to survive the death of Priam and the fall of Troy?

Why does the Earthshaker god (*Ennosigaios*) insist on the survival of this one Trojan hero?

ἀλλ᾽ ἄγεθ᾽ ἡμεῖς πέρ μιν ὑπὲκ θανάτου ἀγάγωμεν,
μή πως καὶ Κρονίδης κεχολώσεται, αἴ κεν Ἀχιλλεὺς
τόνδε κατακτείνῃ: μόριμον δέ οἵ ἐστ᾽ ἀλέασθαι,
ὄφρα μὴ ἄσπερμος γενεὴ καὶ ἄφαντος ὄληται
Δαρδάνου, . . .

But come, let us lead him away from death,
in case the son of Cronus grows enraged if
Achilles kills this man — since the Fates decree
that he escape, to ensure the Dardanian race
does not die out unseen without an heir.

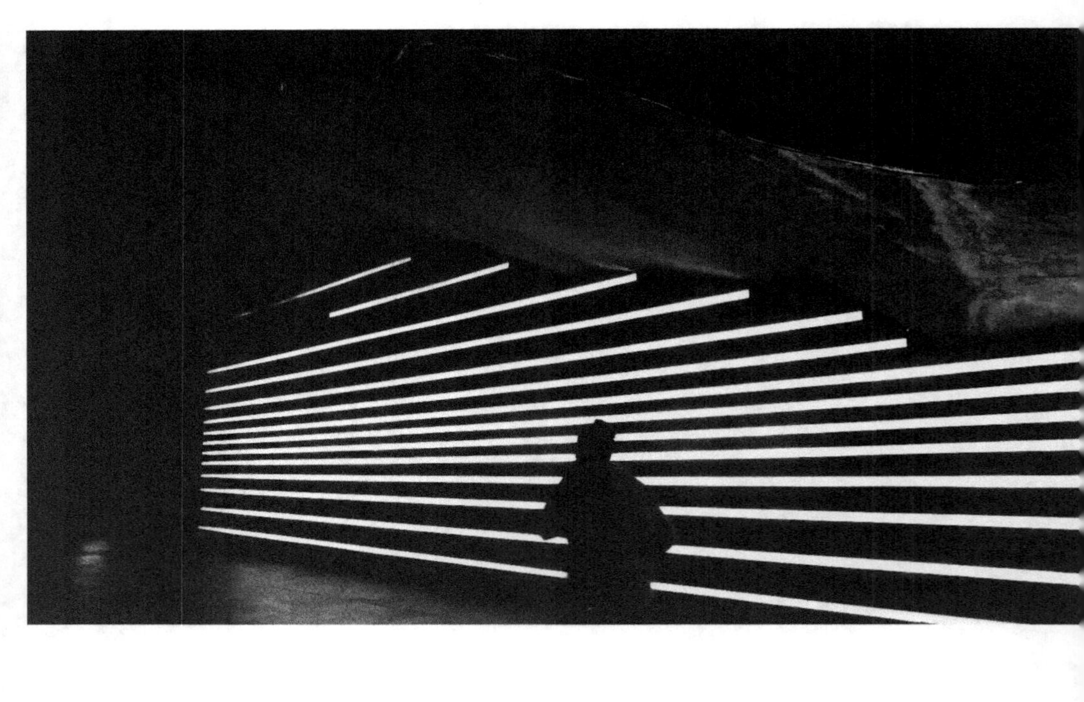

20

Hera cautions Zeus against the temptation to alter fate.

Zeus is the executor of fate, not its author. Perhaps he could defer a fatal outcome. But not even the chief among Olympians can fray the Moirai's thread. So when he sees his son's allotment — when he sees Patroclus closing in on Sarpedon — he grieves.

He acquiesces. Hera stands by him, watching him watch his own son fall.

ἀλλ᾽ εἴ τοι φίλος ἐστί, τεὸν δ᾽ ὀλοφύρεται ἦτορ,
ἤτοι μέν μιν ἔασον ἐνὶ κρατερῇ ὑσμίνῃ
χέρσ᾽ ὕπο Πατρόκλοιο Μενοιτιάδαο δαμῆναι:

But if you do love him and your heart grieves,
let him die in the fierce battle, defeated at
the hand of Patroclus, son of Menoetius.

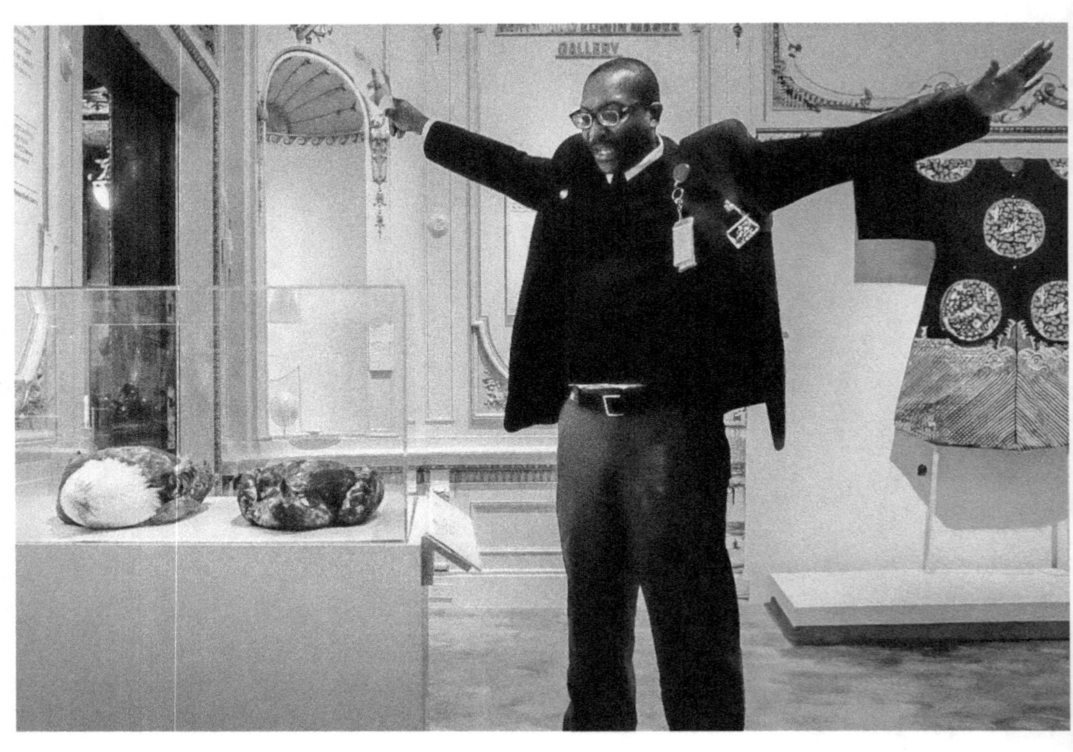

19

Hector refuses the prophecy.

No omen, no sign, no doubt. Ignore the sudden bloodied serpent dropped from the sky. Talons loosed as the enormous snake, carried midflight, strikes the base of the eagle's neck. Dropped into the ranks of Trojan fighters bridging a trench.

Polydamas accosts Hector — the campaign must stop or they will share the eagle's fate.

τύνη δ' οἰωνοῖσι τανυπτερύγεσσι κελεύεις
πείθεσθαι, τῶν οὔ τι μετατρέπομ' οὐδ' ἀλεγίζω
εἴτ' ἐπὶ δεξί' ἴωσι πρὸς ἠῶ τ' ἠέλιόν τε,
εἴτ' ἐπ' ἀριστερὰ τοί γε ποτὶ ζόφον ἠερόεντα.

You ask me to trust in long-winged birds,
but I care nothing for whether they fly on
the right toward the dawn's rising sun, or
fly on the left into misty darkness.

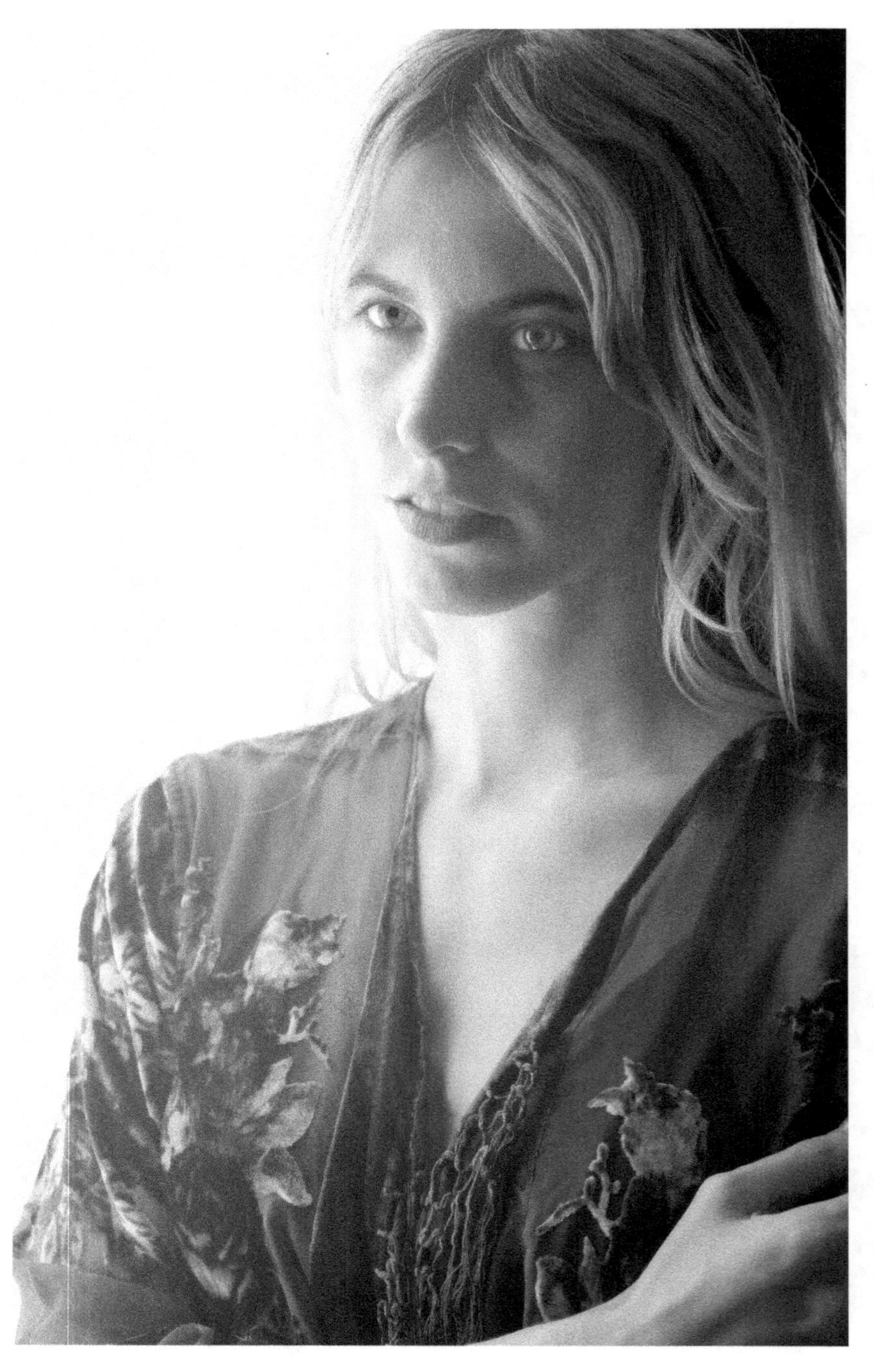

18

She sees them from the heights.

Hermes conceals the king, her father, as he returns with the body of Hector. Cassandra sees them anyway. We know this is her curse. Apollo's revenge resides in her eyes. She has become inured to being disbelieved.

But this time there is no question of belief — it is only the truth that she sees, first, and always.

. . . οὐδέ τις ἄλλος
ἔγνω πρόσθ' ἀνδρῶν καλλιζώνων τε γυναικῶν,
ἀλλ' ἄρα Κασσάνδρη ἰκέλη χρυσῇ Ἀφροδίτῃ
Πέργαμον εἰσαναβᾶσα φίλον πατέρ' εἰσενόησεν
ἑσταότ' ἐν δίφρῳ, κήρυκά τε ἀστυβοώτην:

No one saw them, none among the men, or the women
in their beautiful sashes, before Cassandra, the very
image of golden Aphrodite, who had scaled the slope of
Pergamus and seen her dear father standing in his chariot,
beside the herald whose cries resound throughout the city.

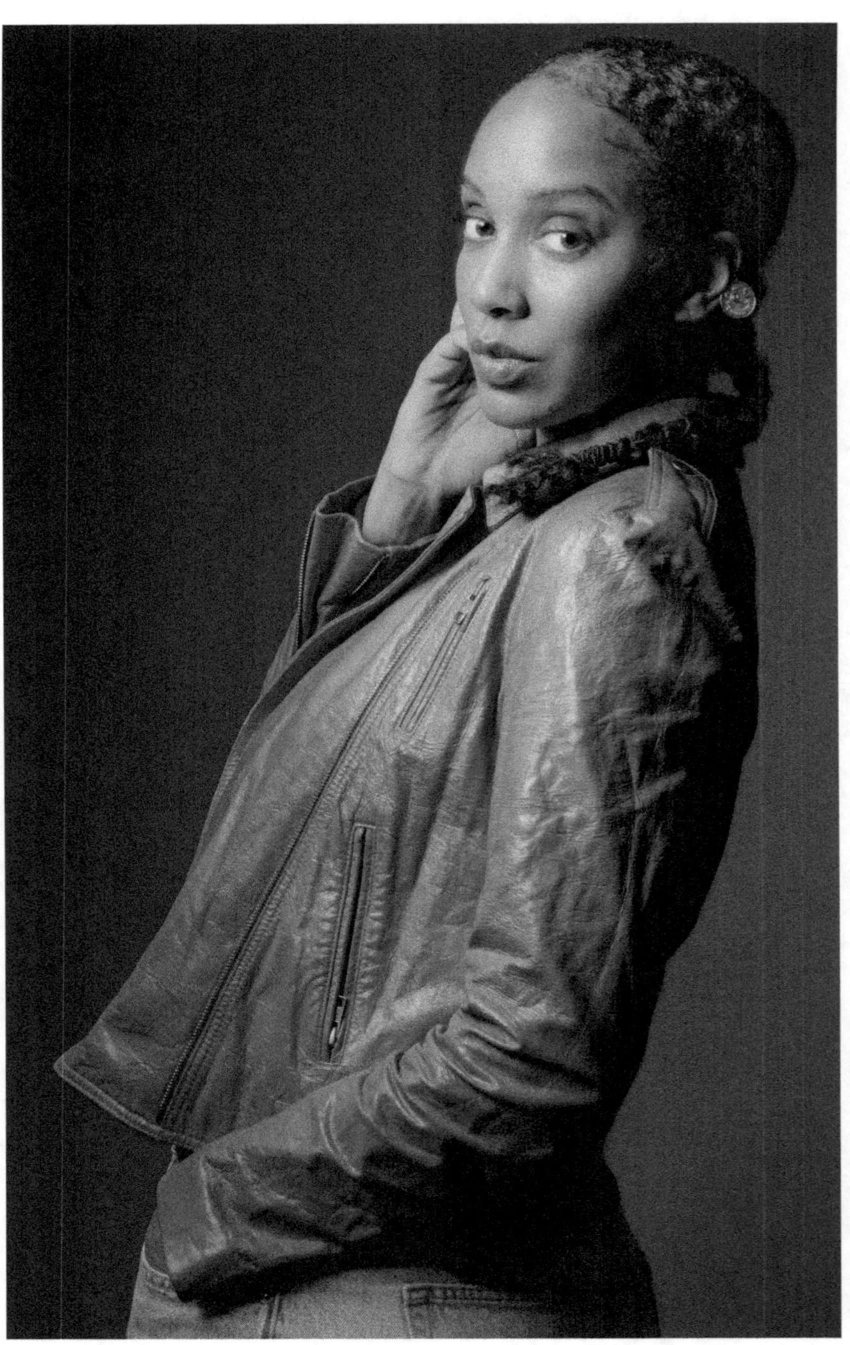

17

Hera will outsmart Zeus.

Distract, deflect, delay, defer. Using his desire to suspend the destruction of her chosen. Let the Argives surge while Zeus lies sated. From Aphrodite, she borrows an enchanted garment. From Hypnos, she coerces stealthy sleep to lay upon the chief of gods.

Once wrapped with Zeus within a golden cloud, she sends along the god of sleep with a message to Poseidon: "Now!"

μερμήριξε δ’ ἔπειτα βοῶπις πότνια Ἥρη
ὅππως ἐξαπάφοιτο Διὸς νόον αἰγιόχοιο:
ἥδε δέ οἱ κατὰ θυμὸν ἀρίστη φαίνετο βουλὴ
ἐλθεῖν εἰς Ἴδην εὖ ἐντύνασαν ἓ αὐτήν,

Then Hera, her eyes ox-wide, began to contrive how she might
outsmart Zeus, the master of the storm-thundering aegis.
In her heart, she decided it was best to deceive him by going to
Mount Ida after making herself resplendent in beauty.

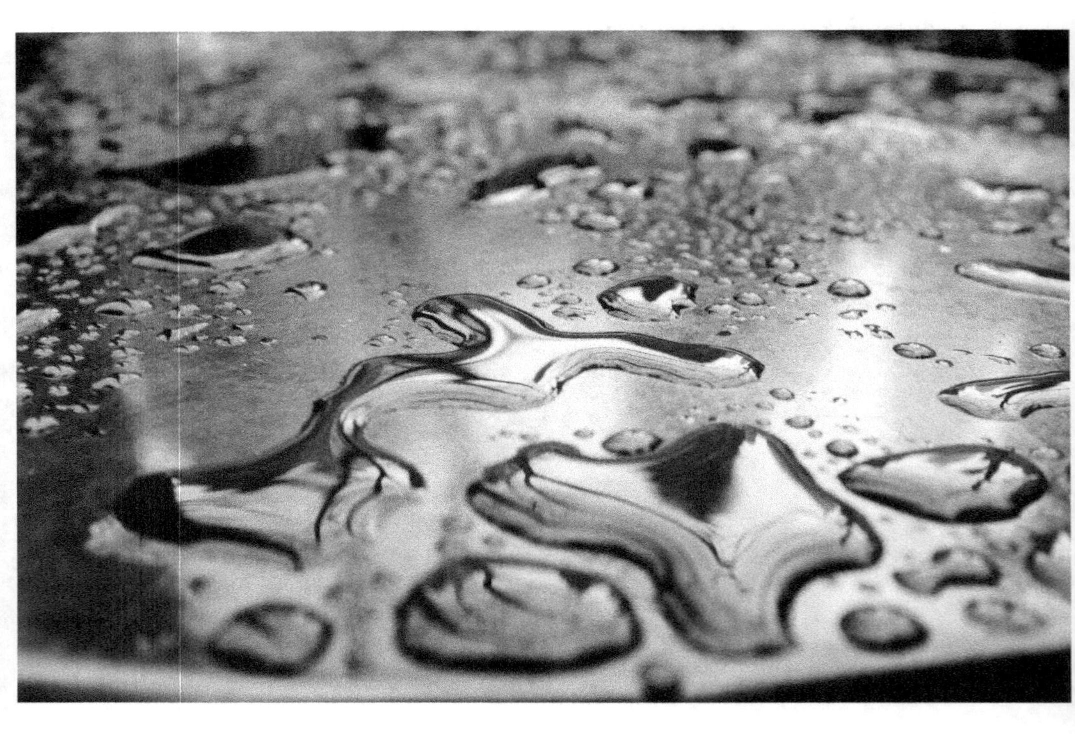

16

Against his better judgment, Achilles allows Patroclus his armor.

Everything except the spear of Pelian ash that only Achilles could cast with precision. Against his better judgment, he places confidence in the sternness of his warning. Drive the Trojans back, then stop and return. Patroclus arms. Achilles raises his cup, pours the libation, and prays.

He puts his faith in Zeus.

ὣς ἔφατ᾽ εὐχόμενος, τοῦ δ᾽ ἔκλυε μητίετα Ζεύς.
τῷ δ᾽ ἕτερον μὲν ἔδωκε πατήρ, ἕτερον δ᾽ ἀνένευσε:
νηῶν μέν οἱ ἀπώσασθαι πόλεμόν τε μάχην τε
δῶκε, σόον δ᾽ ἀνένευσε μάχης ἐξαπονέεσθαι

So in prayer he spoke, and Zeus the counselor heard him.
And the father granted one part and denied the other.
That Patroclus would drive the combat away from the ships
he granted, but safe deliverance from battle he denied him.

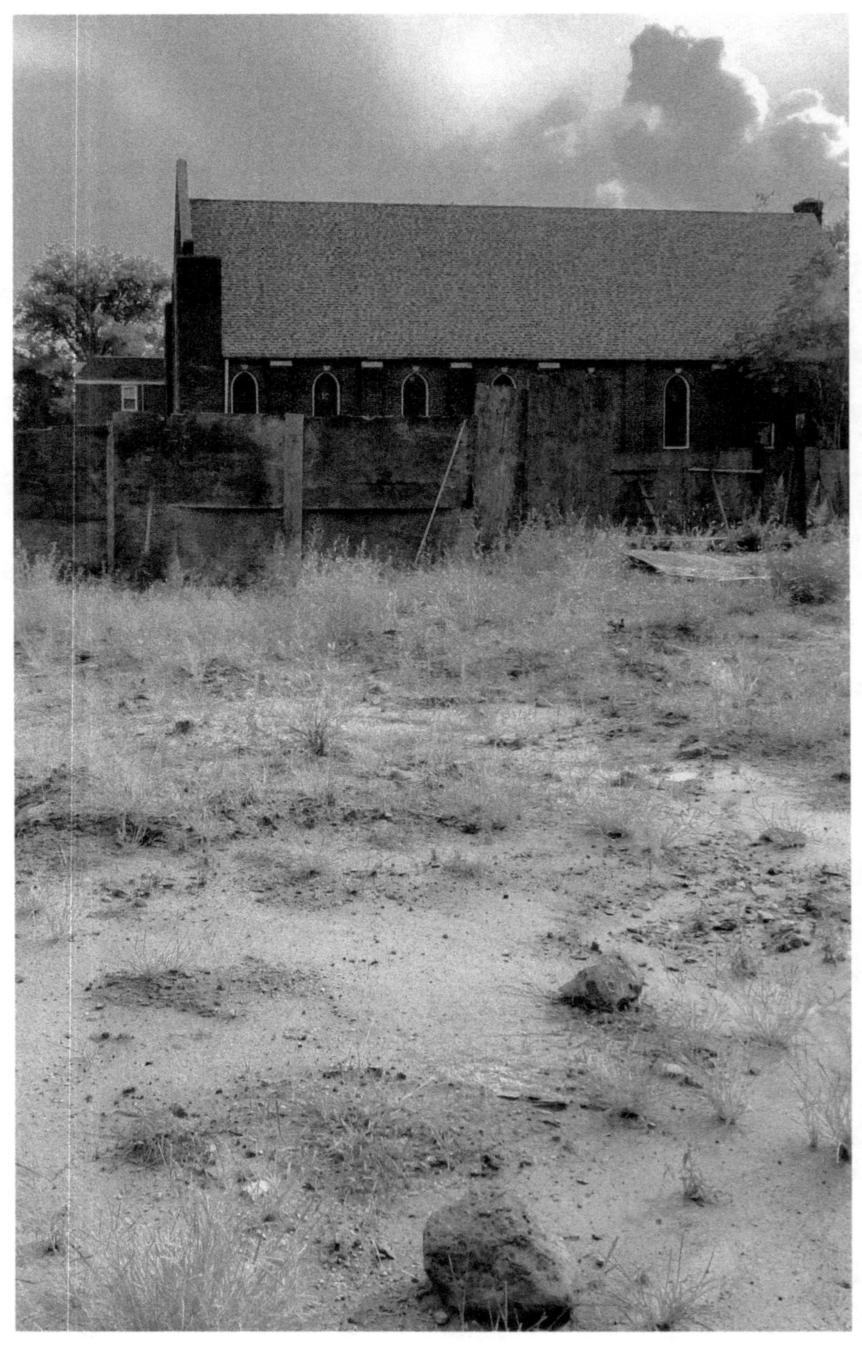

15

Almost all the usages of the word *storm* are figurative. The literal storms are dust storms. Dust kicked airborne by galloping horse-hooves.

But in one instance, Zeus sends down gale winds from Mount Ida. The driven dust batters the Achaean ships. Hector and the Trojans advance that day, ripping ramparts to the ground.

The Argives buttress themselves against the remnants and hold fast. The dust settles into their eyes.

ὣς ἄρα φωνήσας ἡγήσατο, τοὶ δ᾽ ἅμ᾽ ἕποντο
ἠχῇ θεσπεσίῃ· ἐπὶ δὲ Ζεὺς τερπικέραυνος
ὦρσεν ἀπ᾽ Ἰδαίων ὀρέων ἀνέμοιο θύελλαν,
ἥ ῥ᾽ ἰθὺς νηῶν κονίην φέρεν· αὐτὰρ Ἀχαιῶν
θέλγε νόον, Τρωσὶν δὲ καὶ Ἕκτορι κῦδος ὄπαζε.

So he spoke and led the way as they followed in the wake of the deafening thunder that Zeus delights in. And with a sudden blast of wind and dust raised from the Idean slopes, he battered the ships and bewildered Achaean forces, granting glory to the Trojans and Hector.

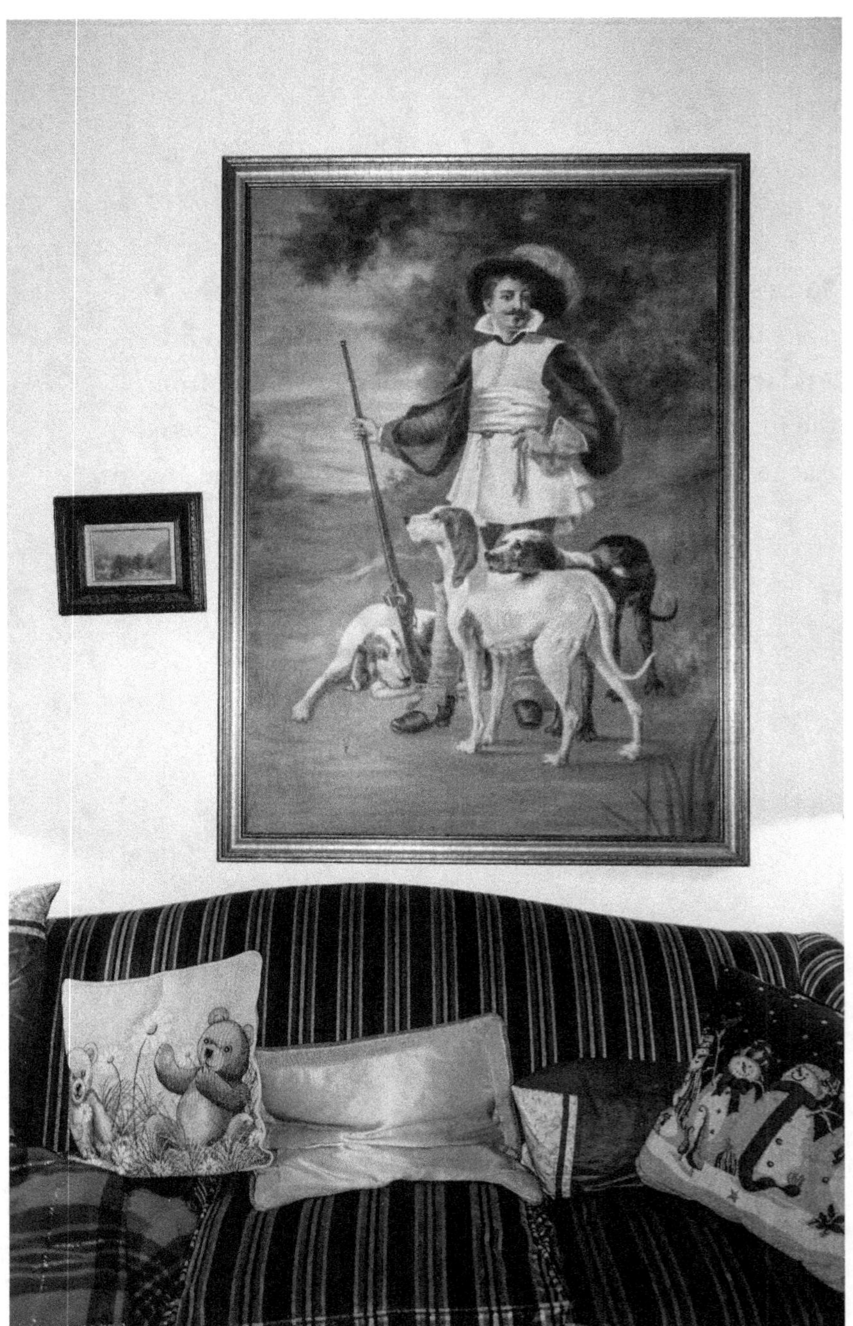

14

Who reads through the Catalogue of Ships? Homer actually lists 1,186 ships. More than Christopher Marlowe's "thousand ships" launched by the face of lovely Helen.

Homer actually lists the contingents of warriors, distinguishes them by their homelands, names their leaders, and numbers their ships. My decision to read the list provided me with a personal payoff. An alphabetical ancestor: A-r-c-e-s-i-laus.

Now I gained an imaginary connection to Troy. Not unlike Mr. Durbeyfield discovering his d'Urbervilles.

Βοιωτῶν μὲν Πηνέλεως καὶ Λήϊτος ἦρχον
Ἀρκεσίλαός τε Προθοήνωρ τε Κλονίος τε,
οἵ θ' Ὑρίην ἐνέμοντο καὶ Αὐλίδα πετρήεσσαν
Σχοῖνόν τε Σκῶλόν τε πολύκνημόν τ' Ἐτεωνόν,

Of the Boeotions, Peneleos and Leitus led the command; Arcesilaus, Prothoënor, and Clonius took charge of men who hailed from Hyria and rocky Aulis, and Schoenus and Scolus and Eteonus, with its many foothills.

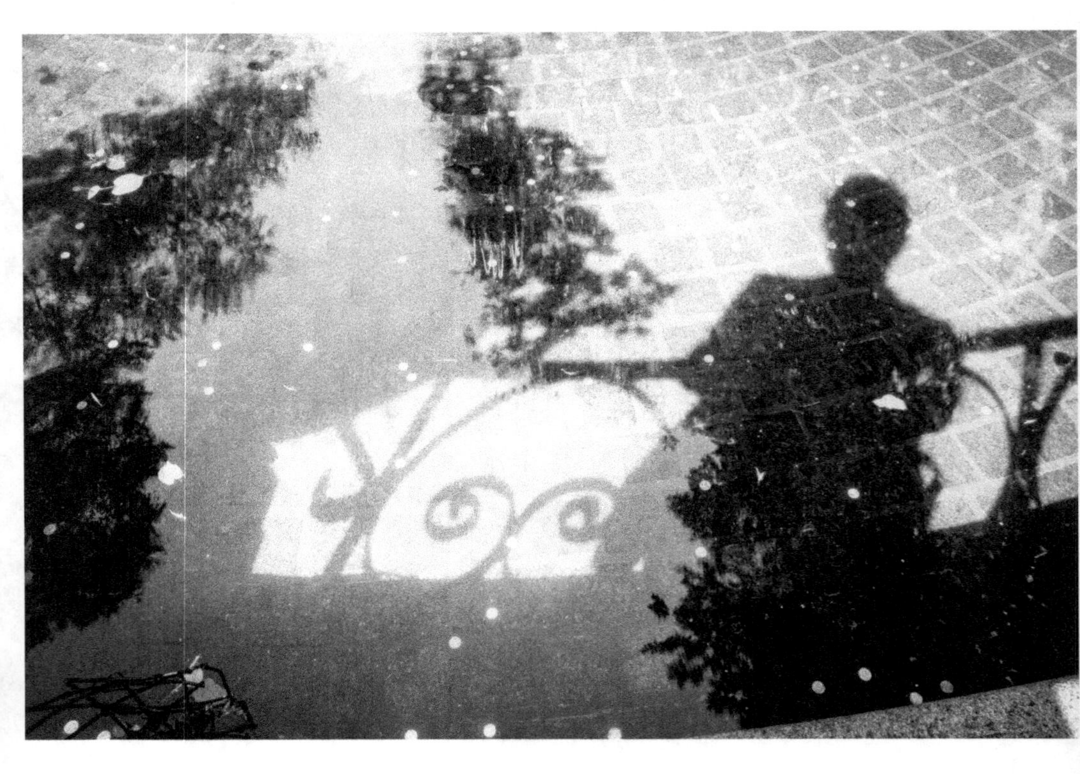

13

We do not think of Hermes as a father.

We are reminded that he is a giant-killer and a guide of dead souls. He is a messenger, and a god of luck. He knows exotic healing herbs. He crosses the boundaries between the world of Olympians, the earth of the mortals, and the underworld. He accompanies and protects Priam on the old king's mission to recover the body of Hector.

Hermes is a father, too, who loved a dancer and whose son commands a ship of Achilles' fleet.

τῆς δ᾽ ἑτέρης Εὔδωρος ἀρήϊος ἡγεμόνευε
παρθένιος, τὸν ἔτικτε χορῷ καλὴ Πολυμήλη
Φύλαντος θυγάτηρ: τῆς δὲ κρατὺς ἀργεϊφόντης
ἠράσατ᾽, ὀφθαλμοῖσιν ἰδὼν μετὰ μελπομένῃσιν
ἐν χορῷ Ἀρτέμιδος χρυσηλακάτου κελαδεινῆς.
αὐτίκα δ᾽ εἰς ὑπερῷ᾽ ἀναβὰς παρελέξατο λάθρῃ

The next brigade was led by fierce Eudorus, the
son of Polymele, unmarried daughter of Phylas,
who birthed him after Hermes the giant-slayer caught
sight of her and lusted as she danced with the girls
in the chorus of Artemis — goddess of golden arrows
and the cry of the hunt.

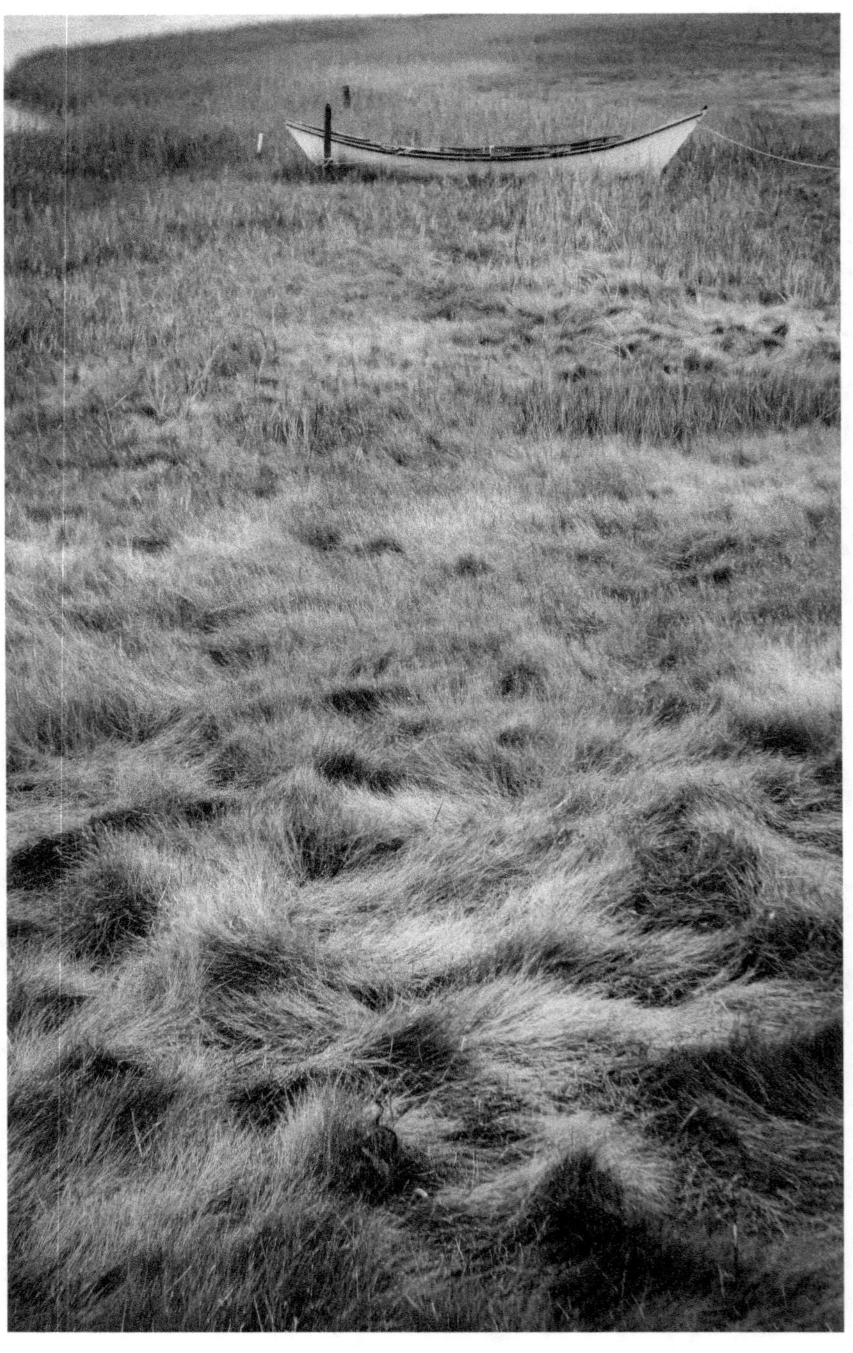

12

The Argives, far from home, have only themselves and their ships to fall back on. Their ramparts torn down, their trenches breached. Prospects bleak with Achilles withdrawn.

Nestor gathers the kings. Agamemnon regrets. Odysseus shames. Diomedes steps forward. That is when Poseidon, watching, decides to intervene. Hera, elated, sees her brother take action. Zeus, her other brother, delays.

The surf rises to the ships. Tides will turn.

πολλὸν γάρ ῥ' ἀπάνευθε μάχης εἰρύατο νῆες
θῖν' ἔφ' ἁλὸς πολιῆς: τὰς γὰρ πρώτας πεδίον δὲ
εἴρυσαν, αὐτὰρ τεῖχος ἐπὶ πρύμνῃσιν ἔδειμαν.
οὐδὲ γὰρ οὐδ' εὐρύς περ ἐὼν ἐδυνήσατο πάσας
αἰγιαλὸς νῆας χαδέειν, στείνοντο δὲ λαοί:
τώ ῥα προκρόσσας ἔρυσαν, καὶ πλῆσαν ἁπάσης
ἠϊόνος στόμα μακρόν, ὅσον συνεέργαθον ἄκραι.

They drew the ships onto the sea's gray shore, far from the clash of battle, with the first wave hauled inland on the plain, and with the sterns they formed a wall. Ship after ship in rows so wide the beach could not contain them all without cramped space between, filling the bay's long mouth between the looming headlands.

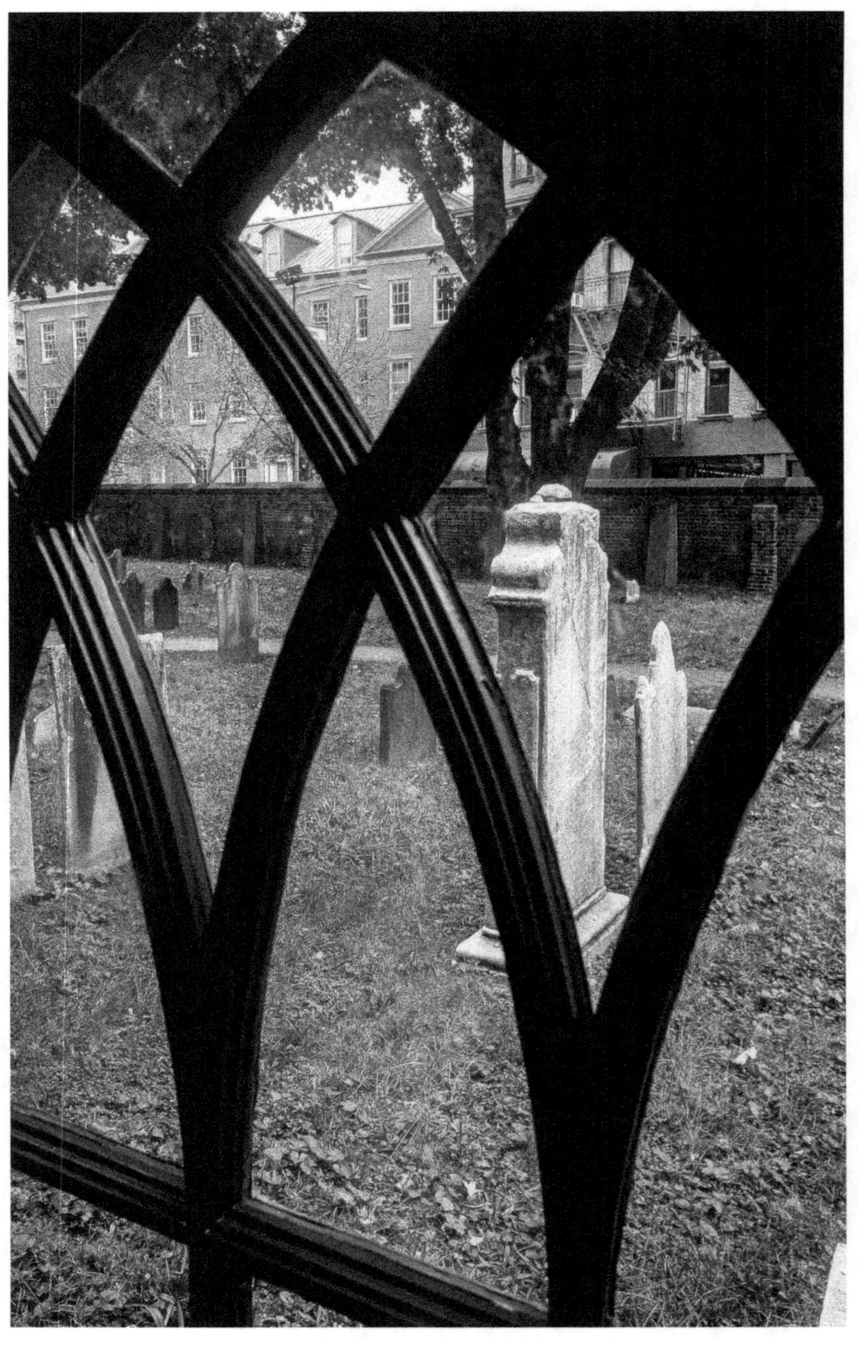

11

This is the heart of the Iliad: that Priam goes to Achilles to recover the body of Hector. It is not a simple matter, and the gods recognize that.

The return of Achilles has devastated gods and mortals — both the deathless and the dying ones. Recall the horror recounted in the invocation. The carrion cost of Achilles' rage. This is what must end with the return of Hector.

To remain unburied is worse than death.

οὐλομένην, ἣ μυρί' Ἀχαιοῖς ἄλγε' ἔθηκε,
πολλὰς δ' ἰφθίμους ψυχὰς Ἄϊδι προΐαψεν
ἡρώων, αὐτοὺς δὲ ἑλώρια τεῦχε κύνεσσιν

That cursed rage which brought down countless catastrophes on the Achaeans, casting heroic souls into Hades, leaving their corpses a feast for carrion and dogs.

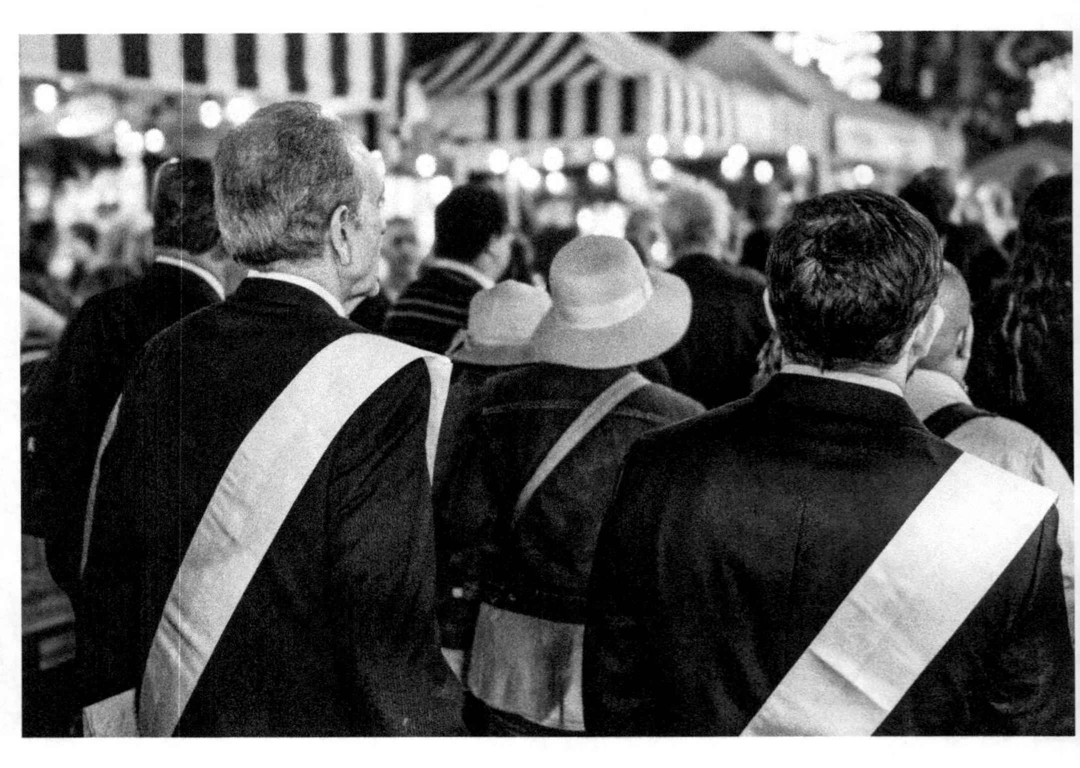

10

After all the scenes of combat.

After all the interference of the gods. After acknowledging the allotments of the Fates. After all, it is just the grief of two men in the tent. Patroclus is dead. Hector is dead. Priam and Achilles speak face to face.

The story will end soon, but the war will continue.

ἀλλ' ἄγε δὴ κατ' ἄρ' ἕζευ ἐπὶ θρόνου ἄλγεα δ' ἔμπης
ἐν θυμῷ κατακεῖσθαι ἐάσομεν ἀχνύμενοί περ
οὐ γάρ τις πρῆξις πέλεται κρυεροῖο γόοιο
ὡς γὰρ ἐπεκλώσαντο θεοὶ δειλοῖσι βροτοῖσι
ζώειν ἀχνυμένοις: αὐτοὶ δέ τ' ἀκηδέες εἰσί

But come now and seat yourself — we will let pain
rest quietly in our hearts despite our grieving,
since there is no gain in the chill of sorrow.
This is what the gods have spun for us mortals:
to live lives of suffering while they live on forever
without cares.

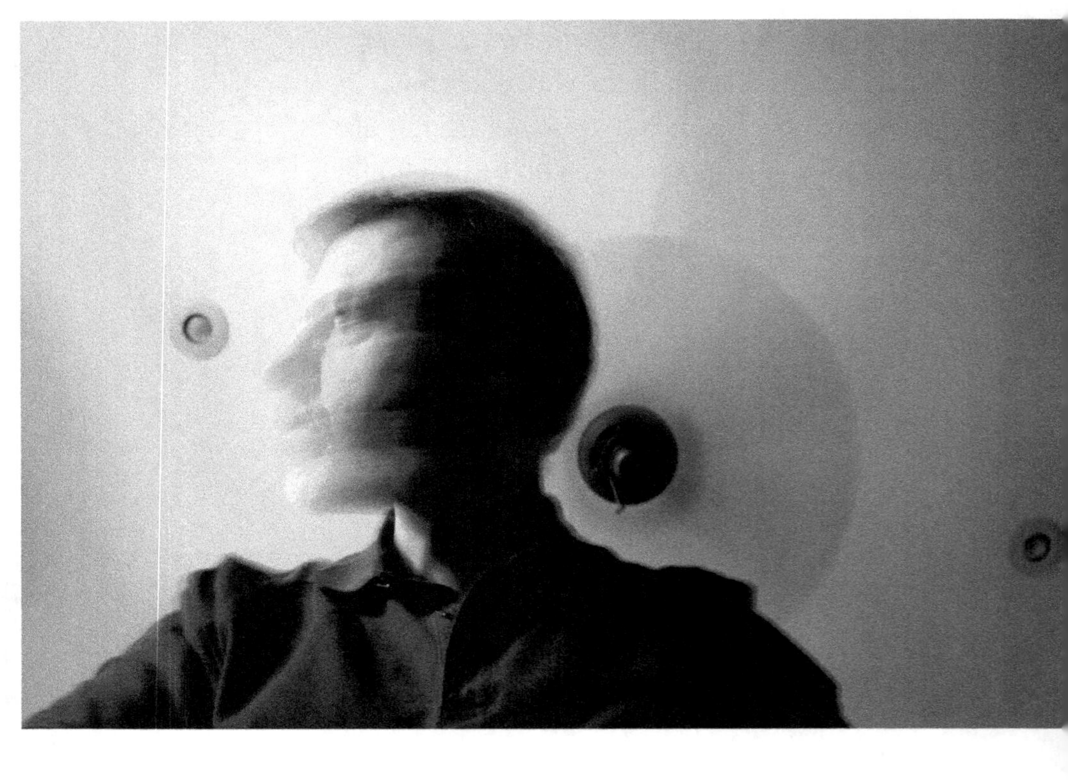

9

Did you ever imagine Priam in the prime of his youth?

Or at any time before the campaign of the Achaeans against Troy? Achilles imagined, as he faced Priam in his tent. Achilles imagined Priam's past as he imagines his own father's future. Peleus, once as gifted as Priam, but with only one son. One son with a dual fate.

Achilles is making his choice as he speaks.

καὶ σὲ γέρον τὸ πρὶν μὲν ἀκούομεν ὄλβιον εἶναι:
ὅσσον Λέσβος ἄνω Μάκαρος ἕδος ἐντὸς ἐέργει
καὶ Φρυγίη καθύπερθε καὶ Ἑλλήσποντος ἀπείρων,
τῶν σε γέρον πλούτῳ τε καὶ υἱάσι φασὶ κεκάσθαι.

And you, old man, they say that you once prospered:
so far as Lesbos, capital of Macar, within your bounds,
and up from Phrygia to the boundless Hellespont,
you surpassed them all, blessed with wealth and sons.

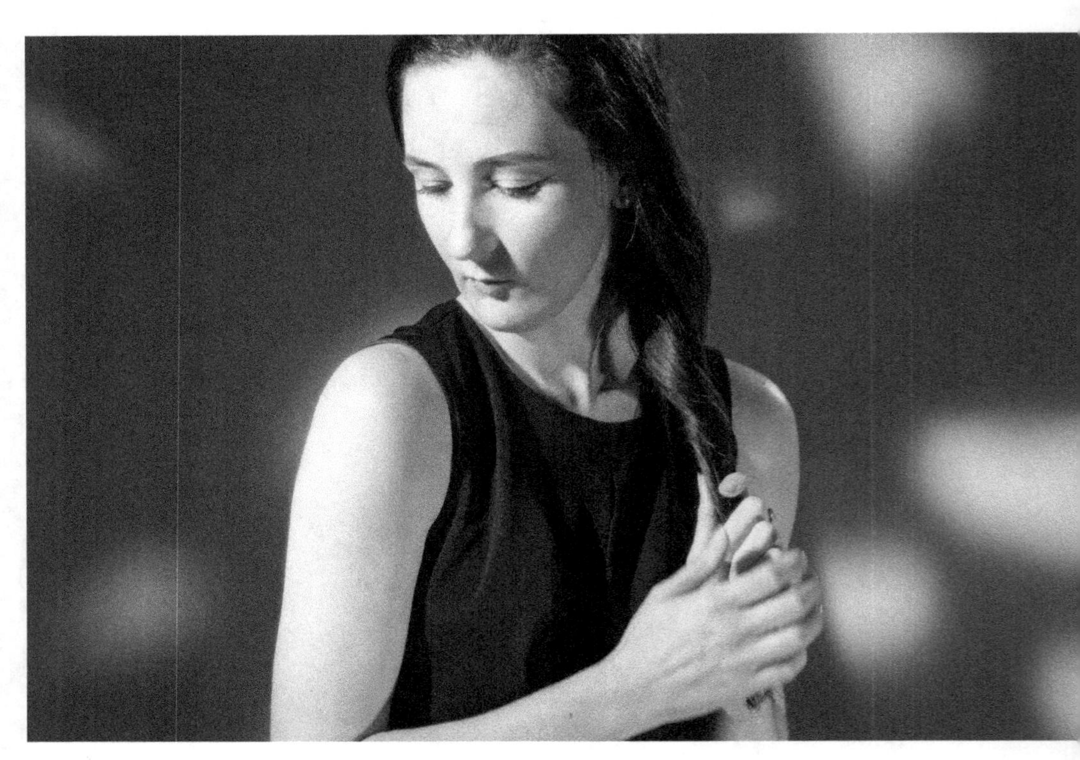

8

Achilles keeps his word to Priam.

Achilles, who moments ago threatened to break the sacred laws of hospitality, returns the body of Hector. He turns to Priam, offering proof, and then offers to share with him the evening meal.

Grief calls for its own protocol, as Achilles recounts the paradigm of Niobe, whose story teaches how to mourn.

υἱὸς μὲν δή τοι λέλυται γέρον ὡς ἐκέλευες,
κεῖται δ᾽ ἐν λεχέεσσ᾽: ἅμα δ᾽ ἠοῖ φαινομένηφιν
ὄψεαι αὐτὸς ἄγων: νῦν δὲ μνησώμεθα δόρπου.
καὶ γάρ τ᾽ ἠΰκομος Νιόβη ἐμνήσατο σίτου,

Your son is laid out on the bier. With the dawn,
you will see for yourself. But for now, let us remember
to sit at supper. Even Niobe with her gleaming hair
Remembered food . . .

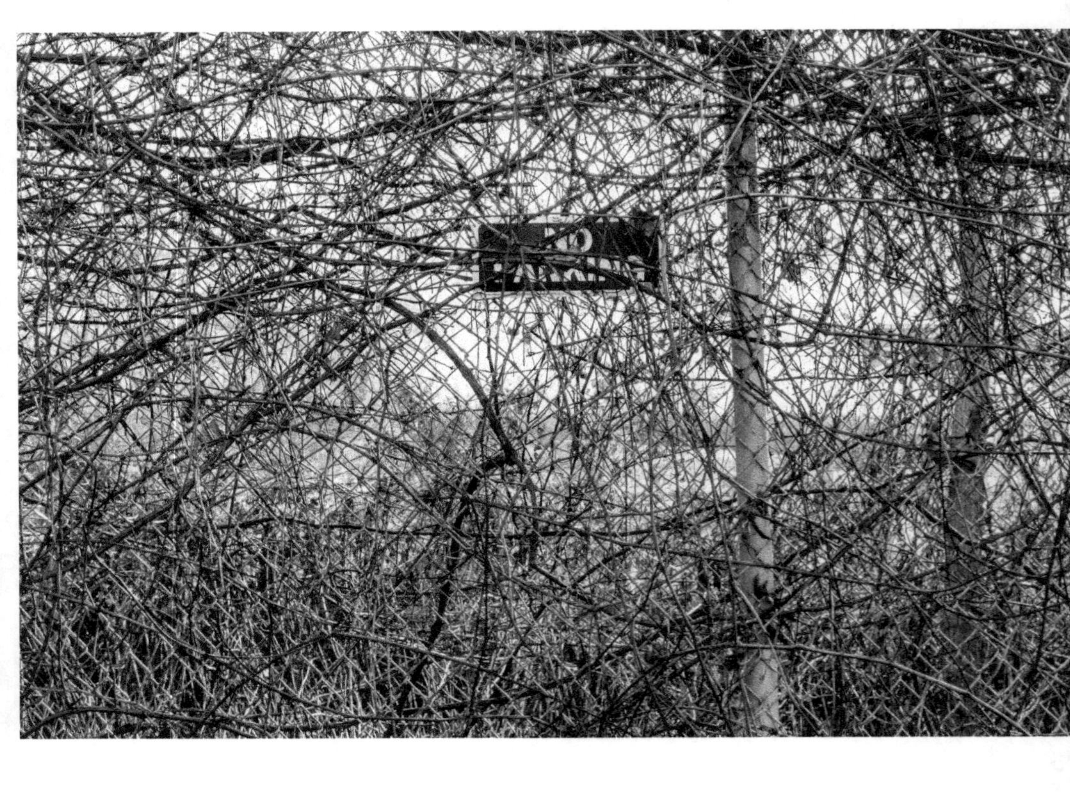
NO

7

An anxious god? Or just a strategist?

Hermes takes care. He led Priam to Achilles and now he must lead him home. Now that the two mortals have settled the terms for Hector's burial.

Hermes loses sleep over Priam.

ἀλλ' οὐχ Ἑρμείαν ἐριούνιον ὕπνος ἔμαρπτεν
ὁρμαίνοντ' ἀνὰ θυμὸν ὅπως Πρίαμον βασιλῆα
νηῶν ἐκπέμψειε λαθὼν ἱεροὺς πυλαωρούς.

But sleep could never hold the running escort,
Hermes kept on turning it over in his mind . . .
how could he convoy Priam clear of the ships,
unseen by devoted guards who held the gates?

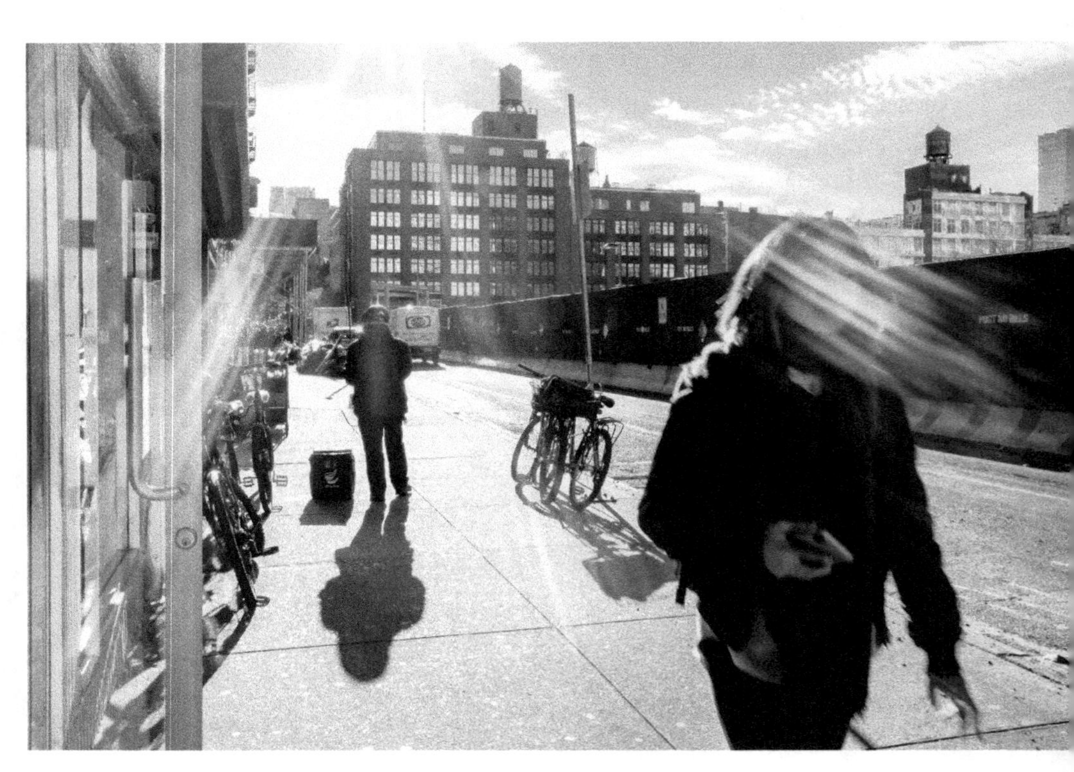

6

Apollo thwarts Achilles.

The god provokes and goads Achilles. He plays decoy, impersonating Angenor. He leads Achilles away in chase and allows the Trojans to retreat behind their walls. Hector still lives at that moment and stands firm by the Scaean Gate.

Apollo cannot stop Achilles, but he can heckle and jeer, he can delay and enrage.

‘τίπτέ με Πηλέος υἱὲ ποσὶν ταχέεσσι διώκεις
αὐτὸς θνητὸς ἐὼν θεὸν ἄμβροτον; οὐδέ νύ πώ με
ἔγνως ὡς θεός εἰμι, σὺ δ’ ἀσπερχὲς μενεαίνεις.

"Why do you pursue me, son of Peleus? Swift as you are, you are still just a mortal chasing down a god. In all your relentless raging, you forget that I am immortal."

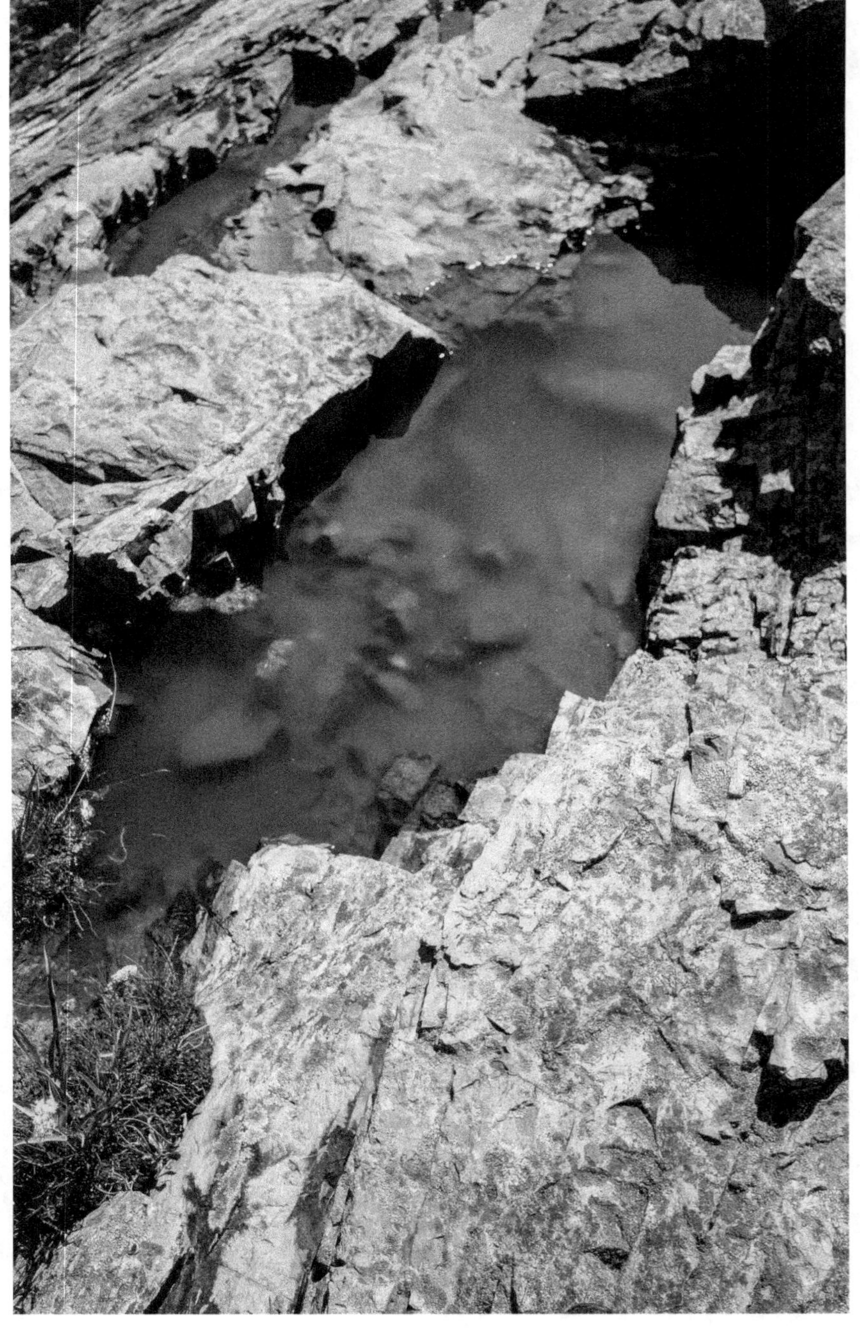

5

Achilles is the fact of terror.

For all of Hector's dignity and courage, there is the fact of fate, and Achilles is that fate. Zeus regrets. Athena warns — Zeus is warned again — against altering fate. But before the chase concludes, there is a moment Homer directs us to.

The clashing heroes pass the now stilled pools, where the Trojan women launder their clothing.

ἔνθα δ' ἐπ' αὐτάων πλυνοὶ εὐρέες ἐγγὺς ἔασι
καλοὶ λαΐνεοι, ὅθι εἵματα σιγαλόεντα
πλύνεσκον Τρώων ἄλοχοι καλαί τε θύγατρες
τὸ πρὶν ἐπ' εἰρήνης πρὶν ἐλθεῖν υἷας Ἀχαιῶν.

And there by the headwaters lay the wide washing-pools of splendid, carved stone where the beautiful wives and daughters of Troy would cleanse their gleaming garments in peacetime, before the Sons of Achaea landed.

4

The gods insist. Zeus summons Thetis to Olympus.

He calls on her to leave the sea, to leave the deep and attend. Her son must give up the body of Hector. He must release. This must come to a close. A mother's word to mitigate unchangeable fate.

She attends, she listens. From the summit she descends to the campground and finds Achilles by the ships.

ἀλλ᾽ ἐμέθεν ξύνες ὦκα, Διὸς δέ τοι ἄγγελός εἰμι:
σκύζεσθαι σοί φησι θεούς, ἓ δ᾽ ἔξοχα πάντων
ἀθανάτων κεχολῶσθαι, ὅτι φρεσὶ μαινομένῃσιν
Ἕκτορ᾽ ἔχεις παρὰ νηυσὶ κορωνίσιν οὐδ᾽ ἀπέλυσας.
ἀλλ᾽ ἄγε δὴ λῦσον, νεκροῖο δὲ δέξαι ἄποινα.

Listen to me — right now! I am bringing you a message straight from Zeus. He says that the gods are enraged, and among the deathless ones, he is especially furious at you for holding back the corpse — and keeping Hector's body unburied beside your ships, out of your heart's spite. Release the body now and accept ransom.

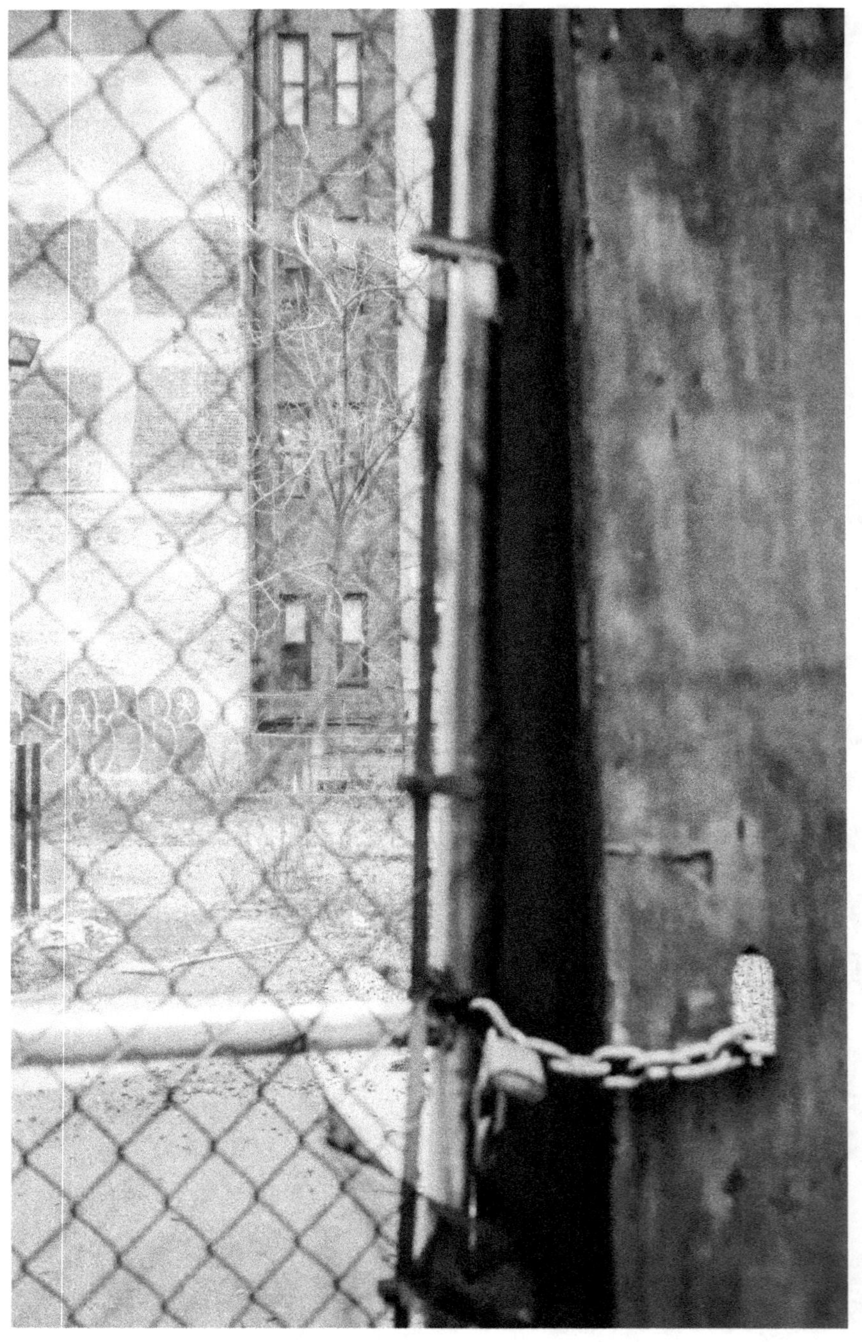

3

Priam is not alone. The gods are always present. Hermes will accompany. He will not set foot in the camp of the mortal, but he will lead one to the other. Face to face. Heartbeat beating to heartbeat. Hermes knows what must be spoken, but the mortals must speak it. Hermes knows that Achilles knows that Peleus will grieve as Priam grieves now.

That's the key — Hermes is, after all, the god of messengers and keys.

ἀλλ' ἤτοι μὲν ἐγὼ πάλιν εἴσομαι, οὐδ' Ἀχιλῆος
ὀφθαλμοὺς εἴσειμι: νεμεσσητὸν δέ κεν εἴη
ἀθάνατον θεὸν ὧδε βροτοὺς ἀγαπαζέμεν ἄντην:
τύνη δ' εἰσελθὼν λαβὲ γούνατα Πηλεΐωνος,
καί μιν ὑπὲρ πατρὸς καὶ μητέρος ἠϋκόμοιο
λίσσεο καὶ τέκεος, ἵνα οἱ σὺν θυμὸν ὀρίνῃς.

But this is as far as I go. I will turn back now, before Achilles sees me. It would only cause an outrage for an immortal to be seen favoring a mortal face to face. But you must go on, kneel and grab his knees, the son of Peleus. Be the supplicant and beg him, by his very own father, by his mother with the flowing hair, and his son — so you will stir his spirit.

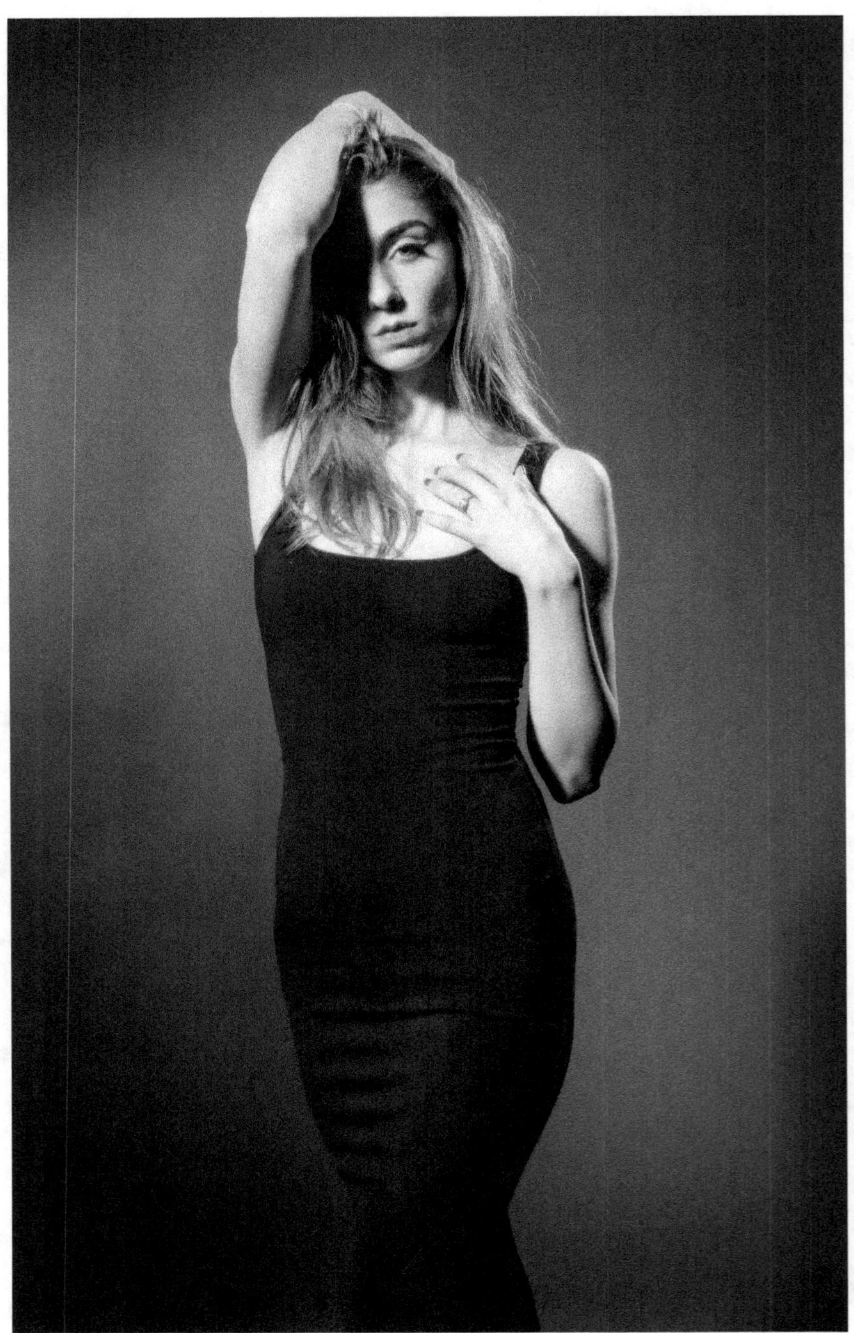

2

Near the very end of the narrative, it is Helen. Helen, whose words are near the last words.

Her portrait of Hector always is one of kindness and dignity up against depravity. Hector has no flaw in this story. He lives life and dies a model of the heroic code. Only the ruinous rage of Achilles provokes Homer to invoke the Muse and sing of disaster. Achilles, the manic demigod, is no match for Hector's human heroism. The fate of Achilles is left for another poem.

This is for Hector. Listen to Helen.

ἀλλ᾽ εἴ τίς με καὶ ἄλλος ἐνὶ μεγάροισιν ἐνίπτοι
δαέρων ἢ γαλόων ἢ εἰνατέρων εὐπέπλων,
ἢ ἑκυρή, ἑκυρὸς δὲ πατὴρ ὣς ἤπιος αἰεί,
ἀλλὰ σὺ τὸν ἐπέεσσι παραιφάμενος κατέρυκες
σῇ τ᾽ ἀγανοφροσύνῃ καὶ σοῖς ἀγανοῖς ἐπέεσσι.

When anyone in the palace would lash out at me, one of your brothers, or sisters, or the wives of your brothers in their luxuriant robes, or even your mother, but never your father, who was always kind as my father to me — but you, you would hold them back, calmly, and with gentle words.

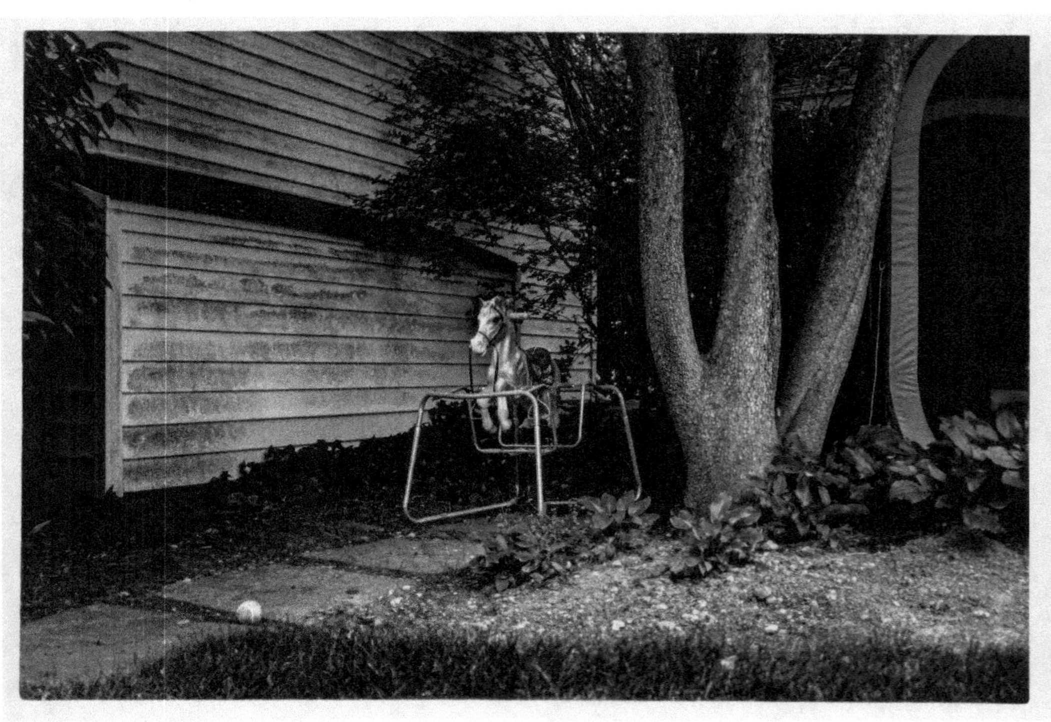

1

What does it mean to be a "breaker of horses"?

Why those last words for Hector? Why the epithet *hippodamos*? Horses are broken for riding and warfare. Only aristocrats break horses. This is the excellence of the Trojans and a mark of Hector as their leader.

It takes nine days to complete the funeral rites. Two or three months more before the fall of Troy.

The ending points beyond the ending.

χεύαντες δὲ τὸ σῆμα πάλιν κίον: αὐτὰρ ἔπειτα
εὖ συναγειρόμενοι δαίνυντ᾽ ἐρικυδέα δαῖτα
δώμασιν ἐν Πριάμοιο διοτρεφέος βασιλῆος.
ὣς οἵ γ᾽ ἀμφίεπον τάφον Ἕκτορος ἱπποδάμοιο.

After they poured heaps of earth into a burial mound,
they returned to the halls of Priam, king raised by Zeus,
and gathered for a glorious funeral feast.
That is how they celebrated Hector, breaker of horses.

Models

Day	Credit
53	Caterina Emma @spirituallystudded
52	Lindsey Waggoner @iamlindseywaggoner
49	Bekah Church @bekahchurch
38	Keryn Huang @kerynhuangvisuals
37	Vinca Minor @vinca_minor
28	Melissa Gaudet @melissaisnumber1
18	Cat Yudain @catyudaintea
17	Cherice Marie @chericemarieartist
8	Erica @erica.nyc
2	Brooke Henry @bookaboutbrooke

Iliad References

Day	Book and lines
54	01.345-50
53	03.153-57
52	03.177-80
51	01.359-60
50	08.562-65
49	03.424-27
48	05.337-42
47	06.146-49
46	02.185-87
45	09.157-59
44	11.670-71
43	05.773-76
42	11.01-02
41	13.10-14
40	16.30-32
39	21.305-08
38	06.293-95
37	03.121-24
36	05.447-48
35	24.718-20
34	10.82-85
33	01.465-68

Day	Book and lines
32	06.354-58
31	18.491-93
30	18.607-10
29	18.587-89
28	18.590-92
27	18.569-72
26	06.402-04
25	06.431-36
24	06.447-49
23	06.472-73
22	20.158-60
21	20.300-05
20	16.450-52
19	12.237-40
18	24.697-701
17	14.159-62
16	16.249-52
15	12.251-55
14	02.494-97
13	16.179-84
12	14.30-36
11	01.02-04

Day	Book and lines
10	24.522-26
09	24.543-46
08	24.599-603
07	24.679-81
06	22.08-10
05	22.153-56
04	24.133-37
03	24.462.67
02	24.767-72
01	24.801-04

Note on the Text

The Greek text of the *Iliad* used in this volume is based on the digital edition available through the Perseus Digital Library at Tufts University: https://www.perseus.tufts.edu/hopper/

Source edition: Homer. *Homeri Opera* in five volumes. Oxford: Oxford University Press, 1920.

- View the Greek text:
  https://www.perseus.tufts.edu/hopper/text?doc=Perseus%3Atext%3A1999.01.0133

- CTS catalog entry:
  http://data.perseus.org/catalog/urn:cts:greekLit:tlg0012.tlg001.perseus-grc1

This digital edition is made available by the Perseus Project under a Creative Commons Attribution-ShareAlike 3.0 United States License.

The selections used here have been excerpted and reformatted for this volume.

Acknowledgments

Thanks to the teachers who helped me see in words and pictures.

Janusz Kawa, Andrew Lichtenstein, Karen Marshall, Jacques Menasche, Sister Patricia McCarthy, Sister Mary Verity McNicholas, Stacy Mehrfar, Walter James Miller, William Packard, Barron Rachman, Brian Rose, and Michael Silverwise.

About the Author

Peter Arcese is a writer, photographer, and teacher whose work explores the enduring resonance of classical literature in the modern world. For over twenty-five years, he has taught classic and contemporary literature at New York University. His poetry and translations have appeared in the *New York Quarterly* and the *Gallatin Review*, and he is the translator of Aeschylus's *Agamemnon* into syllabic verse. His photography, rooted in documentary and poetic traditions, was included in the International Center of Photography's *Concerned: Images of Social Distancing* project and published in the accompanying book. He lives and works in New York, where he continues to pursue projects that draw connections across time, language, and expression.

www.ingramcontent.com/pod-product-compliance
Lightning Source LLC
LaVergne TN
LVHW020711110826
845149LV00012B/2203

* 9 7 9 8 9 9 1 9 5 8 5 2 3 *